THE MEANING OF
CONTEMPORARY REALISM

THE MEANING OF
CONTEMPORARY REALISM

Georg Lukács

TRANSLATED FROM THE GERMAN BY
John and Necke Mander

London

MERLIN PRESS

PRINTED IN GREAT BRITAIN BY
WHITSTABLE LITHO LTD,
WHITSTABLE, KENT.
AND FIRST PUBLISHED IN ENGLAND
IN THIS TRANSLATION 1963 BY
MERLIN PRESS LTD.,
3 MANCHESTER ROAD, LONDON,
ENGLISH TRANSLATION COPYRIGHT © 1963
BY MERLIN PRESS LTD
SECOND IMPRESSION 1969
THIRD IMPRESSION 1972
FOURTH IMPRESSION 1979

ISBN 085036 250 4

Contents

Preface to the English Edition

I⊤ IS now five years since this book was first written. In the meantime many of the tendencies noted in it have been confirmed; the text, therefore, requires no major alteration. I have made a brief addition (p. 83), illustrating the applicability of my general thesis to some other contemporary writers. That 'loss of authenticity' which I noted in modernist literature, while a gradual and complex process, does not seem to have been halted. And the same is true of the remnants of Stalinism in the socialist countries. The XXIInd Congress has here reinforced the shock of the XXth: dogmatic sectarianism has abandoned open opposition and been forced on to the defensive. Resistance now takes the form of assertions—despite lip-service to the decisions of the XXIInd Congress—that everything is in excellent order, that no further critique of Stalinism is needed, no return to the unpolluted sources of Marxism, no re-adjustment of the arts and sciences to present-day requirements.

The combating of these tendencies is a practical rather than a theoretical task, since the dogmatists prefer to shelter behind their bureaucratic entrenchment, reluctant to engage in sober argument. Nevertheless, the effort to rid the movement of the disastrous legacy of Stalinism—and to rediscover the creative core of the teaching of Marx, Engels, and Lenin—remains our most urgent task. Much of value has already been done. Thus, two years ago the Soviet magazine *Drushba Narodov* (1960, No. 4) published a hitherto unknown letter of Krupskaya's, in which she declares that Lenin's famous 1905 essay *Party Organisation and Party Literature* was *not* concerned with literature as fine art—a view I have long held. The importance of this statement is considerable, for this essay was the bible of sectarianism in the

7

arts during the ideological dictatorship of Stalin and Zhdanov. It is curious, and interesting, that the publication of Krupskaya's letter should have received so little attention.

No less interesting is a passage in a speech by Tvardovsky, the well-known Soviet writer, at the XXIInd Congress, where he sharply attacks what I call in this book 'illustrative literature'. The phrase is, in fact, in both cases a quotation. That intelligent and courageous critic of the Thirties, E. Ussiyevitch, published at that period an essay *Against Illustrative Literature* which caused an uproar in the dogmatic sectarian camp. The instance is of more than historical interest. It will come to be appreciated that a section of the editorial staff of the magazine *Literaturny Kritik* was engaged during the Thirties in a tenacious underground struggle against the dogmatism that dominated literary criticism at the time. The theoretical implications of this are of some topicality.

One could point to many other, similar instances. But it is general developments, not individual instances, that concern us here. These developments suggest to me that my book, no less than when it was first composed has the character of a polemic. They also suggest that it may soon—the sooner the better—acquire the character of an historical document.

Budapest, May 1962.

Preface to the German Edition

THE FOLLOWING study was composed in the autumn of 1955 as the basis of lectures given at the *Deutsche Akademie der Künste* in Berlin, at the Academy for Social Sciences in Warsaw, at the universities of Rome, Florence, Bologna, Turin, and Milan and, finally, to the Urania Society in Vienna. For reasons of brevity, I restricted myself to one main problem—the position of bourgeois realism in capitalist society—though the latter part of the study already existed in rough draft.

Lecturing and writing are very different activities. Writing the lectures up, I realized I would have to include rather more illustrative material than had been possible in the lectures; though I decided to preserve the essay form and eschew a systematic approach. Reading the latter part of this study it must be borne in mind that I wrote it immediately after the XXth Congress of the Soviet Communist Party. I would like to emphasize this point. Readers of my earlier work will be aware that this study contains no ideas I have not expressed elsewhere. This should be evident from my discussion of naturalism and schematism. Verbally new, perhaps, is my polemic against 'revolutionary romanticism'. But only verbally. During the two decades when the term 'revolutionary romanticism' was in vogue I never used it, either in writing or in conversation. I tried to show that the problems of literary criticism could be solved better without it. More direct opposition was impossible while Stalin was alive and the reign of Zhdanov absolute. That my silence was taken for opposition is proved by the fact that I was blamed for refusing to mention this 'revolutionary romanticism'. I am happy to take this opportunity to discuss the question openly, no longer in 'Aesopean language'. It will be clear to readers of my earlier work that there has been no basic change in my views. I would like, however, to discuss this terminological question fully and frankly at this point.

I began this preface in September 1956. In the meantime, in Hungary and other countries, events have occurred which demand a rethinking of certain problems connected with Stalin's legacy. In the bourgeois world (and, in some instances, in the socialist countries) this reaction has taken the form of a revision of the theories of Marx and Lenin. It is no doubt correct to see in revisionism the main danger facing Marxism-Leninism at present. But we will be helpless in the face of this danger unless we are prepared to submit Stalin's own dogmatism, and that of the Stalinist period, to the most relentless criticism. We must demonstrate the underlying pattern common to both, and the similarity of method. And we must isolate those elements in both which are contradictory to Marxism-Leninism. Only on the basis of such criticism, as with Rosa Luxemburg's complex legacy, can Stalin's positive achievements be seen in perspective. Since, however, the present study is only concerned with one—though a central—aspect of this whole complex, we can dispense with a general theoretical discussion.

Yet, though I deal here with only one aspect of contemporary literature, my treatment of it is not without relation to more general problems. In the discussions following the XXth Congress, a parallel revisionism sprang up in the field of literary criticism which rejected both the Marxist concepts of 'decadence' and of 'socialist realism'—branding this last as obstructive of cultural progress. There are still, on the other hand, the dogmatists, who attempt to defend everything—'except a few mistakes'—that occurred during the last decades. Here, too, I would put forward a *tertium datur*. For we cannot neutralize revisionism—the greatest present danger for Marxism, I repeat—without an energetic critique of dogmatism. The emergence of a new style is apparent in the works of writers like Sholokhov and Makarenko. But if every mediocre product of socialist realism is to be hailed as a masterpiece, confusion will be worse con-

10

founded. My *tertium datur* is an objective critical appraisal of the very real innovations which we owe to socialist realism. In exposing literary mediocrity, and criticizing theoretical dogmatism, I am trying to ensure that the creative aspects of this new realism be more clearly understood.

Budapest, April 1957.

Introduction

LET US begin by examining two prejudices. The first is typical of much present-day bourgeois criticism. It is contained in the proposition that the literature of 'modernism', of the *avantgarde*, is the essentially modern literature. The traditional techniques of realism, these critics assert, are inadequate, because too superficial, to deal with the realities of our age. On the other hand, there are not a few exponents of socialist realism who assert that the emergence of socialist realism has rendered bourgeois 'critical realism' obsolete. The trouble with both these approaches—diametrically opposed as they are—is that they are based on a monolithic view of modern bourgeois literature, and neglect significant aspects of our social, and thus of our cultural and literary, life.

Both approaches, of course, are deeply rooted in the social conditions of our time. The struggle between socialism and capitalism is still—as it has been since the 1848 rising of the Paris proletariat—the fundamental reality of the modern age. We would expect literature and criticism to reflect this reality. But this does not imply that every work of art, every cultural event, is directly determined by it. The formative principle of an age manifests itself in devious ways. In a larger perspective, the struggle between capitalism and socialism may be the formative principle of our age. But to relate day-to-day phenomena, or even longer-term trends, *directly* to this struggle can well be misleading.

Before the Second World War, for example, it was not this conflict that determined the social and political pattern, but the conflict between Fascism and anti-Fascism. It is true that some forces within capitalism—represented by Hitler, but also by

13

bourgeois politicians—were interested to emphasize the more fundamental division. But to no purpose. The conflict between Fascism and anti-Fascism was more dynamic and the more immediate. It determined the social and political pattern of a large part of mankind during that decisive phase. After Hitler's defeat it seemed—from the time, say, of Churchill's Fulton speech—as if the struggle between socialism and capitalism was once more to dominate the scene. The strategists of the Cold War aimed to divide mankind into two hostile camps and to mobilize all non-socialist forces against socialism. Once more, to no purpose. New forces unexpectedly emerged, which were to assume great importance. These forces were opposed to policies leading to the outbreak of the Third World War. This is not the place to outline the growth of the Peace Movement. It is enough to say that the movement came to comprise hundreds of millions of people—a mass movement without parallel in history.

A closer look at these two great alliances of recent history reveals that both the bourgeois camp, and to a lesser degree the proletarian, were divided. Just as there were workers who were misled by Fascism, so there are workers today who fall for Cold War ideology. For the purposes of this study, however, it is far more significant that both the anti-Fascist cause and the Peace Movement attracted large sections of the bourgeoisie, and particularly of the bourgeois intelligentsia. The struggle between capitalism and socialism was, in fact, not directly relevant to either. Indeed, both movements were characterized by a militant alliance between socialist and bourgeois forces.

This had important consequences for modern bourgeois literature. And a closer examination of the ideological character of the Peace Movement reveals still other aspects. The point I am making is no less true of the anti-Fascist movement, though it is less striking there. It is highly significant that the main presupposition of the Peace Movement is the bracketing-out of ideological differences. Marxists and supporters of bourgeois ideologies, atheists and members of the most diverse religions, all belong to it; and differences of ideology have not proved an obstacle to the closest co-operation.

The situation is, in fact, even more complex. The practical activities of the Peace Movement often raise questions of an ideological character. Nobody can work effectively for peace unless he is firmly convinced that society is amenable to the processes of reason and that human effort—in terms of individual, as well as mass action—*can* influence historical events. Equally, a belief in the inevitability of war, in the destruction of civilization by nuclear warfare, is often rooted in philosophical fatalism. Thus the polarization of opinion brought about by the Peace Movement is not without its ideological elements. But these elements are ideological only in the narrow sense of the word. They are simply the common denominator which people of differing, even opposed, attitudes of mind must share if they are determined to act together. It may imply no more than a superficial awareness of certain problems and a practical reaction to them. This awareness itself may be expressed in terms of different, even contradictory, philosophical or religious systems. Fatalism may have its roots in pseudo-scientific, or in religious, modes of thought. Equally, a belief in reason, in individual responsibility, may be grounded in a theological or a materialist theory of society. The common ideological factor is thus, in Hegel's phrase, 'an identity of identity and non-identity'.

It is no exaggeration to say that this new principle determining human allegiances is the starting-point of my investigation. For this kind of awareness is characteristic precisely of the artist's apprehension of reality. A work of art may be unequivocal in content and structure and yet open to differing, even contradictory, interpretations. For us, this identity—an identity which goes to the root of the matter—is of supreme importance. For it reveals that, all divergencies apart, a common social attitude does indeed exist.

Our starting-point, then, is really the point of convergence of two antitheses: the antithesis between realism and modernism and the antithesis between peace and war. Yet, while emphasizing this identity, certain reservations must be made. The identity in question is essentially abstract. In individual cases it will appear in many differing, transitional forms. Indeed, it is of the essence of this complex problem that no strict polarization exists. It would be oversimplifying the matter to identify opposing or converging tendencies with individual movements or personalities. These tendencies are often to be found in one and the same individual. They are to be found, not only as discrete stages in his development, but as co-existent at one and the same time, expressive of those contradictions characteristic of his stage of development.

Here, as so often, knowledge of the present illuminates the past. We see clearly that what is happening today is the outcome of hidden, but long active forces. The 'great realism' of the first half of the nineteenth century was followed by a period of relative mediocrity after 1848 (the age of Napoleon II, the first years of the Third Republic, the later Victorian period). And we see, too, that the gathering economic tempest of the early years of imperialism gave rise to a new realism: it led to a 'humanist revolt' against imperialism. The national roots of this movement are extremely various; the stylistic expressions still more so. All the more striking then, seen from the perspective of our time, is the common ideological basis of this 'humanist revolt'. It is only necessary to look at writers like Anatole France and Romain Rolland, Shaw and Dreiser, Heinrich and Thomas Mann to see what I mean by this common basis. Contemporary bourgeois realism—many of whose exponents span the modern period—represents, essentially, a continuation of this revolt.

The Ideology of Modernism

IT IS in no way surprising that the most influential contemporary school of writing should still be committed to the dogmas of 'modernist' anti-realism. It is here that we must begin our investigation if we are to chart the possibilities of a bourgeois realism. We must compare the two main trends in contemporary bourgeois literature, and look at the answers they give to the major ideological and artistic questions of our time.

We shall concentrate on the underlying ideological basis of these trends (ideological in the above-defined, not in the strictly philosophical, sense). What must be avoided at all costs is the approach generally adopted by bourgeois-modernist critics themselves: that exaggerated concern with formal criteria, with questions of style and literary technique. This approach may appear to distinguish sharply between 'modern' and 'traditional' writing (i.e. contemporary writers who adhere to the styles of the last century). In fact it fails to locate the decisive formal problems and turns a blind eye to their inherent dialectic. We are presented with a false polarization which, by exaggerating the importance of stylistic differences, conceals the opposing principles actually underlying and determining contrasting styles.

To take an example: the *monologue intérieur*. Compare, for instance, Bloom's monologue in the lavatory or Molly's monologue in bed, at the beginning and at the end of *Ulysses*, with Goethe's early-morning monologue as conceived by Thomas Mann in his *Lotte in Weimar*. Plainly, the same stylistic technique is being employed. And certain of Thomas Mann's remarks about Joyce and his methods would appear to confirm this.

Yet it is not easy to think of any two novels more basically dissimilar than *Ulysses* and *Lotte in Weimar*. This is true even

17

of the superficially rather similar scenes I have indicated. I am not referring to the—to my mind—striking difference in intellectual quality. I refer to the fact that with Joyce the stream-of-consciousness technique is no mere stylistic device; it is itself the formative principle governing the narrative pattern and the presentation of character. Technique here is something absolute; it is part and parcel of the aesthetic ambition informing *Ulysses*. With Thomas Mann, on the other hand, the *monologue intérieur* is simply a technical device, allowing the author to explore aspects of Goethe's world which would not have been otherwise available. Goethe's experience is not presented as confined to momentary sense-impressions. The artist reaches down to the core of Goethe's personality, to the complexity of his relations with his own past, present, and even future experience. The stream of association is only apparently free. The monologue is composed with the utmost artistic rigour: it is a carefully plotted sequence gradually piercing to the core of Goethe's personality. Every person or event, emerging momentarily from the stream and vanishing again, is given a specific weight, a definite position, in the pattern of the whole. However unconventional the presentation, the compositional principle is that of the traditional epic; in the way the pace is controlled, and the transitions and climaxes are organized, the ancient rules of epic narration are faithfully observed.

It would be absurd, in view of Joyce's artistic ambitions and his manifest abilities, to qualify the exaggerated attention he gives to the detailed recording of sense-data, and his comparative neglect of ideas and emotions, as artistic failure. All this was in conformity with Joyce's artistic intentions; and, by use of such techniques, he may be said to have achieved them satisfactorily. But between Joyce's intentions and those of Thomas Mann there is a total opposition. The perpetually oscillating patterns of sense- and memory-data, their powerfully charged—but aimless and directionless—fields of force, give rise to an epic structure which is *static*, reflecting a belief in the basically static character of events.

These opposed views of the world—dynamic and developmental on the one hand, static and sensational on the other—are of crucial importance in examining the two schools of literature I have mentioned. I shall return to the opposition later. Here, I want only to point out that an exclusive emphasis on formal matters can lead to serious misunderstanding of the character of an artist's work.

What determines the style of a given work of art? How does the intention determine the form? (We are concerned here, of course, with the intention realized in the work; it need not coincide with the writer's conscious intention). The distinctions that concern us are not those between stylistic 'techniques' in the formalistic sense. It is the view of the world, the ideology or *weltanschauung* underlying a writer's work, that counts. And it is the writer's attempt to reproduce this view of the world which constitutes his 'intention' and is the formative principle underlying the style of a given piece of writing. Looked at in this way, style ceases to be a formalistic category. Rather, it is rooted in content; it is the specific form of a specific content.

Content determines form. But there is no content of which Man himself is not the focal point. However various the *données* of literature (a particular experience, a didactic purpose), the basic question is, and will remain: what is Man?

Here is a point of division: if we put the question in abstract, philosophical terms, leaving aside all formal considerations, we arrive—for the realist school—at the traditional Aristotelian dictum (which was also reached by other than purely aesthetic considerations): Man is *zoon politikon*, a social animal. The Aristotelian dictum is applicable to all great realistic literature. Achilles and Werther, Oedipus and Tom Jones, Antigone and Anna Karenina: their individual existence—their *Sein an sich*, in the Hegelian terminology; their 'ontological being', as a more fashionable terminology has it—cannot be distinguished from their social and historical environment. Their human significance, their specific individuality cannot be separated from the context in which they were created.

19

The ontological view governing the image of man in the work of leading modernist writers is the exact opposite of this. Man, for these writers, is by nature solitary, asocial, unable to enter into relationships with other human beings. Thomas Wolfe once wrote: 'My view of the world is based on the firm conviction that solitariness is by no means a rare condition, something peculiar to myself or to a few specially solitary human beings, but the inescapable, central fact of human existence.' Man, thus imagined, may establish contact with other individuals, but only in a superficial, accidental manner; only, ontologically speaking, by retrospective reflection. For 'the others', too, are basically solitary, beyond significant human relationship.

This basic solitariness of man must not be confused with that individual solitariness to be found in the literature of traditional realism. In the latter case, we are dealing with a particular situation in which a human being may be placed, due either to his character or to the circumstances of his life. Solitariness may be objectively conditioned, as with Sophocles' Philoctetes, put ashore on the bleak island of Lemnos. Or it may be subjective, the product of inner necessity, as with Tolstoy's Ivan Ilyitsch or Flaubert's Frédéric Moreau in the *Education Sentimentale*. But it is always merely a fragment, a phase, a climax or anti-climax, in the life of the community as a whole. The fate of such individuals is characteristic of certain human types in specific social or historical circumstances. Beside and beyond their solitariness, the common life, the strife and togetherness of other human beings, goes on as before. In a word, their solitariness is a specific social fate, not a universal *condition humaine*.

The latter, of course, is characteristic of the theory and practice of modernism. I would like, in the present study, to spare the reader tedious excursions into philosophy. But I cannot refrain from drawing the reader's attention to Heidegger's description of human existence as a 'thrownness-into-being' (*Geworfenheit ins Dasein*). A more graphic evocation of the ontological solitariness of the individual would be hard to imagine. Man is 'thrown-into-being'. This implies, not merely that man is constitutionally unable to establish relationships with things or persons outside himself; but also that it is impossible to determine theoretically the origin and goal of human existence.

Man, thus conceived, is an ahistorical being. (The fact that Heidegger does admit a form of 'authentic' historicity in his system is not really relevant. I have shown elsewhere that Heidegger tends to belittle historicity as 'vulgar'; and his 'authentic' historicity is not distinguishable from ahistoricity). This negation of history takes two different forms in modernist literature. First, the hero is strictly confined within the limits of his own experience. There is not for him—and apparently not for his creator—any pre-existent reality beyond his own self, acting upon him or being acted upon by him. Secondly, the hero himself is without personal history. He is 'thrown-into-the-world': meaninglessly, unfathomably. He does not develop through contact with the world; he neither forms nor is formed by it. The only 'development' in this literature is the gradual revelation of the human condition. Man is now what he has always been and always will be. The narrator, the examining subject, is in motion; the examined reality is static.

Of course, dogmas of this kind are only really viable in philosophical abstraction, and then only with a measure of sophistry. A gifted writer, however extreme his theoretical modernism, will in practice have to compromise with the demands of historicity and of social environment. Joyce uses Dublin, Kafka and Musil the Hapsburg Monarchy, as the locus of their masterpieces. But the locus they lovingly depict is little more than a backcloth; it is not basic to their artistic intention.

This view of human existence has specific literary consequences. Particularly in one category, of primary theoretical and practical importance, to which we must now give our attention: that of *potentiality*. Philosophy distinguishes between *abstract* and *concrete* (in Hegel, 'real') *potentiality*. These two categories, their interrelation and opposition, are rooted in life itself. *Potentiality*—seen abstractly or subjectively—is richer than actual life. Innumerable possibilities for man's development are imaginable, only a small percentage of which will be realized. Modern subjectivism, taking these imagined possibilities for actual complexity of life, oscillates between melancholy and fascination. When the world declines to realize these possibilities, this melancholy becomes tinged with contempt. Hofmannsthal's Sobeide expressed the reaction of the generation first exposed to this experience:

> The burden of those endlessly pored-over
> And now forever perished possibilities . . .

How far were those possibilities even concrete or 'real'? Plainly, they existed only in the imagination of the subject, as dreams or day-dreams. Faulkner, in whose work this subjective potentiality plays an important part, was evidently aware that reality must thereby be subjectivized and made to appear arbitrary. Consider this comment of his: 'They were all talking simultaneously, getting flushed and excited, quarrelling, making the unreal into a possibility, then into a probability, then into an irrefutable fact, as human beings do when they put their wishes into words.' The possibilities in a man's mind, the particular pattern, intensity and suggestiveness they assume, will of course be characteristic of that individual. In practice, their number will border on the infinite, even with the most unimaginative individual. It is thus a hopeless undertaking to define the contours of individuality, let alone to come to grips with a man's actual fate, by means of potentiality. The *abstract* character of potentiality is clear from the fact that it cannot determine development—subjective mental states, however permanent or profound, cannot here be decisive. Rather, the development of personality is determined by inherited gifts and qualities; by the factors, external or internal, which further or inhibit their growth.

But in life potentiality can, of course, become reality. Situations arise in which a man is confronted with a choice; and in the act of choice a man's character may reveal itself in a light that surprises even himself. In literature—and particularly in dramatic literature—the denouement often consists in the realization of just such a potentiality, which circumstances have kept from coming to the fore. These potentialities are, then, 'real' or concrete potentialities. The fate of the character depends upon the potentiality in question, even if it should condemn him to a tragic end. In advance, while still a subjective potentiality in the character's mind, there is no way of distinguishing it from the innumerable abstract potentialities in his mind. It may even be buried away so completely that, before the moment of decision, it has never entered his mind even as an abstract potentiality. The subject, after taking his decision, may be unconscious of his own motives. Thus Richard Dudgeon, Shaw's Devil's Disciple, having sacrificed himself as Pastor Andersen, confesses: 'I have often asked myself for the motive, but I find no good reason to explain why I acted as I did.'

Yet it is a decision which has altered the direction of his life. Of course, this is an extreme case. But the qualitative leap of the denouement, cancelling and at the same time renewing the continuity of individual consciousness, can never be predicted. The concrete potentiality cannot be isolated from the myriad abstract potentialities. Only actual decision reveals the distinction.

The literature of realism, aiming at a truthful reflection of reality, must demonstrate both the concrete and abstract potentialities of human beings in extreme situations of this kind. A character's concrete potentiality once revealed, his abstract potentialities will appear essentially inauthentic. Moravia, for instance, in his novel *The Indifferent Ones*, describes the young son of a decadent bourgeois family, Michel, who makes up his mind to kill his sister's seducer. While Michel, having made his decision, is planning the murder, a large number of abstract—but highly suggestive—possibilities are laid before us. Unfortunately for Michel the murder is actually carried out; and, from the sordid details of the action, Michel's character emerges as what it is—representative of that background from which, in subjective fantasy, he had imagined he could escape.

Abstract potentiality belongs wholly to the realm of subject-

23

tivity; whereas concrete potentiality is concerned with the dialectic between the individual's subjectivity and objective reality. The literary presentation of the latter thus implies a description of actual persons inhabiting a palpable, identifiable world. Only in the interaction of character and environment can the concrete potentiality of a particular individual be singled out from the 'bad infinity' of purely abstract potentialities, and emerge as the determining potentiality of just this individual at just this phase of his development. This principle alone enables the artist to distinguish concrete potentiality from a myriad abstractions.

But the ontology on which the image of man in modernist literature is based invalidates this principle. If the 'human condition'—man as a solitary being, incapable of meaningful relationships—is identified with reality itself, the distinction between abstract and concrete potentiality becomes null and void. The categories tend to merge. Thus Cesare Pavese notes with John Dos Passos, and his German contemporary, Alfred Döblin, a sharp oscillation between 'superficial *verisme*' and 'abstract Expressionist schematism'. Criticizing Dos Passos, Pavese writes that fictional characters 'ought to be created by deliberate selection and description of individual features'—implying that Dos Passos' characterizations are transferable from one individual to another. He describes the artistic consequences: by exalting man's subjectivity, at the expense of the objective reality of his environment, man's subjectivity itself is impoverished.

The problem, once again, is ideological. This is not to say that the ideology underlying modernist writings is identical in all cases. On the contrary: the ideology exists in extremely various, even contradictory forms. The rejection of narrative objectivity, the surrender to subjectivity, may take the form of Joyce's stream of consciousness, or of Musil's 'active passivity', his 'existence without quality', or of Gide's '*action gratuite*', where abstract potentiality achieves pseudo-realization. As individual character manifests itself in life's moments of decision, so too in literature. If the distinction between abstract and concrete potentiality

24

vanishes, if man's inwardness is identified with an abstract subjectivity, human personality must necessarily disintegrate.

T. S. Eliot described this phenomenon, this mode of portraying
human personality, as

> Shape without form, shade without colour,
> Paralysed force, gesture without motion.

The disintegration of personality is matched by a disintegration
of the outer world. In one sense, this is simply a further consequence of our argument. For the identification of abstract and
concrete human potentiality rests on the assumption that the
objective world is inherently inexplicable. Certain leading
modernist writers, attempting a theoretical apology, have admitted this quite frankly. Often this theoretical impossibility of
understanding reality is the point of departure, rather than the
exaltation of subjectivity. But in any case the connection between the two is plain. The German poet Gottfried Benn, for
instance, informs us that 'there is no outer reality, there is only
human consciousness, constantly building, modifying, rebuild-
ing new worlds out of its own creativity'. Musil, as always, gives
a moral twist to this line of thought. Ulrich, the hero of his *The
Man without Qualities*, when asked what he would do if he
were in God's place, replies: 'I should be compelled to abolish
reality.' Subjective existence 'without qualities' is the complement of the negation of outward reality.

The negation of outward reality is not always demanded with
such theoretical rigour. But it is present in almost all modernist
literature. In conversation, Musil once gave as the period of his
great novel, 'between 1912 and 1914'. But he was quick to modify
this statement by adding: 'I have not, I must insist, written a
historical novel. I am not concerned with actual events. . . .
Events, anyhow, are interchangeable. I am interested in what is
typical, in what one might call the ghostly aspect of reality.'
The word 'ghostly' is interesting. It points to a major tendency
in modernist literature: the attenuation of actuality. In Kafka,
the descriptive detail is of an extraordinary immediacy and

authenticity. But Kafka's artistic ingenuity is really directed towards substituting his *angst*-ridden vision of the world for objective reality. The realistic detail is the expression of a ghostly un-reality, of a nightmare world, whose function is to evoke *angst*. The same phenomenon can be seen in writers who attempt to combine Kafka's techniques with a critique of society—like the German writer, Wolfgang Koeppen, in his satirical novel about Bonn, *Das Treibhaus*. A similar attenuation of reality underlies Joyce's stream of consciousness. It is, of course, intensified where the stream of consciousness is itself the medium through which reality is presented. And it is carried *ad absurdum* where the stream of consciousness is that of an abnormal subject or of an idiot—consider the first part of Faulkner's *Sound and Fury* or, a still more extreme case, Beckett's *Molloy*.

Attenuation of reality and dissolution of personality are thus interdependent: the stronger the one, the stronger the other. Underlying both is the lack of a consistent view of human nature. Man is reduced to a sequence of unrelated experiential fragments; he is as inexplicable to others as to himself. In Eliot's *Cocktail Party* the psychiatrist, who voices the opinions of the author, describes the phenomenon:

> Ah, but we die to each other daily
> What we know of other people
> Is only our memory of the moments
> During which we knew them. And they have changed
> $\qquad\qquad\qquad\qquad\qquad$ since then.
> To pretend that they and we are the same
> Is a useful and convenient social convention
> Which must sometimes be broken. We must also remember
> That at every meeting we are meeting a stranger.

The dissolution of personality, originally the unconscious product of the identification of concrete and abstract potentiality, is elevated to a deliberate principle in the light of consciousness. It is no accident that Gottfried Benn called one of his theoretical tracts 'Doppelleben'. For Benn, this dissolution of personality took the form of a schizophrenic dichotomy. According to him, there was in man's personality no coherent pattern of motivation or behaviour. Man's animal nature is opposed to his denaturized, sublimated thought-processes. The unity of thought and action is 'backwoods philosophy'; thought and being are 'quite separate entities'. Man must be either a moral or a thinking being—he cannot be both at once.

These are not, I think, purely private, eccentric speculations. Of course, they are derived from Benn's specific experience. But there is an inner connection between these ideas and a certain tradition of bourgeois thought. It is more than a hundred years since Kierkegaard first attacked the Hegelian view that the inner and outer world form an objective dialectical unity, that they are indissolubly married in spite of their apparent opposition. Kierkegaard denied any such unity. According to Kierkegaard, the individual exists within an opaque, impenetrable 'incognito'.

This philosophy attained remarkable popularity after the Second World War—proof that even the most abstruse theories may reflect social reality. Men like Martin Heidegger, Ernst Jünger, the lawyer Carl Schmitt, Gottfried Benn and others passionately embraced this doctrine of the eternal incognito which implies that a man's external deeds are no guide to his motives. In this case, the deeds obscured behind the mysterious incognito were, needless to say, these intellectuals' participation in Nazism: Heidegger, as Rector of Freiburg University, had glorified Hitler's seizure of power at his Inauguration; Carl Schmitt had put his great legal gifts at Hitler's disposal. The facts were too well-known to be simply denied. But, if this impenetrable incognito were the true 'condition humaine', might not—concealed within their incognito—Heidegger or Schmitt have been secret opponents of Hitler all the time, only supporting him in the world of appearances? Ernst von Salomon's cynical frankness about his opportunism in The Questionnaire (keeping his reservations to himself or declaring them only in the presence of intimate friends) may be read as an ironic commentary on this ideology of the incognito as we find it, say, in the writings of Ernst Jünger.

This digression may serve to show, taking an extreme example, what the social implications of such an ontology may be. In the literary field, this particular ideology was of cardinal importance; by destroying the complex tissue of man's relations with his environment, it furthered the dissolution of personality. For it is just the opposition between a man and his environment that determines the development of his personality. There is no great hero of fiction—from Homer's Achilles to Mann's Adrian Leverkühn or Sholochov's Grigory Melyekov—whose personality is not the product of such an opposition. I have shown how disastrous the denial of the distinction between abstract and concrete potentiality must be for the presentation of character. The destruction of the complex tissue of man's interaction with his environment likewise saps the vitality of this opposition. Certainly, some writers who adhere to this ideology have attempted, not unsuccessfully, to portray this opposition in concrete terms. But the underlying ideology deprives these contradictions of their dynamic, developmental significance. The contradictions co-exist, unresolved, contributing to the further dissolution of the personality in question.

It is to the credit of Robert Musil that he was quite conscious of the implications of his method. Of his hero Ulrich he remarked: 'One is faced with a simple choice: either one must run with the pack (when in Rome, do as the Romans do); or one becomes a neurotic.' Musil here introduces the problem, central to all modernist literature, of the significance of psychopathology.

This problem was first widely discussed in the Naturalist period. More than fifty years ago, that doyen of Berlin dramatic critics, Alfred Kerr, was writing: 'Morbidity is the legitimate poetry of Naturalism. For what is poetic in everyday life? Neurotic aberration, escape from life's dreary routine. Only in this way can a character be translated to a rarer clime and yet retain an air of reality.' Interesting, here, is the notion that the poetic necessity of the pathological derives from the prosaic quality of life under capitalism. I would maintain—we shall return to this point—that in modern writing there is a continuity from Naturalism to the Modernism of our day—a continuity restricted, admittedly, to underlying ideological principles. What at first was no more than dim anticipation of approaching catastrophe developed, after 1914, into an all-pervading obsession. And I would suggest that the ever-increasing part played by psychopathology was one of the main features of the continuity. At each period—depending on the prevailing social and historical conditions—psychopathology was given a new emphasis, a different significance and artistic function. Kerr's description suggests that in naturalism the interest in psychopathology sprang from an aesthetic need; it was an attempt to escape from the dreariness of life under capitalism. The quotation from Musil shows that some years later the opposition acquired a moral slant. The obsession with morbidity had ceased to have a merely decorative function, bringing colour into the greyness of reality, and become a moral protest against capitalism.

With Musil—and with many other modernist writers—psychopathology became the goal, the *terminus ad quem*, of their artistic intention. But there is a double difficulty inherent in their intention, which follows from its underlying ideology. There is, first, a lack of definition. The protest expressed by this flight into psychopathology is an abstract gesture; its rejection of reality is wholesale and summary, containing no concrete criticism. It is a gesture, moreover, that is destined to lead nowhere; it is an escape into nothingness. Thus the propagators of this ideology are mistaken in thinking that such a protest could ever be fruitful in literature. In any protest against particular social conditions, these conditions themselves must have the central place. The bourgeois protest against feudal society, the proletarian against bourgeois society, made their point of departure a criticism of the old order. In both cases the protest—reaching out beyond the point of departure—was based on a concrete *terminus ad quem*: the establishment of a new order. However indefinite the structure and content of this new order, the will towards its more exact definition was not lacking.

How different the protest of writers like Musil! The *terminus a quo* (the corrupt society of our time) is inevitably the main source of energy, since the *terminus ad quem* (the escape into psychopathology) is a mere abstraction. The rejection of modern reality is purely subjective. Considered in terms of man's relation with his environment, it lacks both content and direction. And this lack is exaggerated still further by the character of the *terminus ad quem*. For the protest is an empty gesture, expressing nausea, or discomfort, or longing. Its content—or rather lack of content—derives from the fact that such a view of life cannot impart a sense of direction. These writers are not wholly wrong in believing that psychopathology is their surest refuge; it is the ideological complement of their historical position.

This obsession with the pathological is not only to be found in literature. Freudian psychoanalysis is its most obvious expression. The treatment of the subject is only superficially different from that in modern literature. As everybody knows, Freud's starting point was 'everyday life'. In order to explain 'slips' and day-dreams, however, he had to have recourse to psychopathology. In his lectures, speaking of resistance and repression, he says: 'Our interest in the general psychology of symptom-formation increases as we understand to what extent the study of pathological conditions can shed light on the workings of the normal mind.' Freud believed he had found the key to the understanding of the normal personality in the psychology of the abnormal. This belief is still more evident in the typology of Kretschmer, which also assumes that psychological abnormalities can explain normal psychology. It is only when we compare Freud's psychology with that of Pavlov, who takes the Hippocratic view that mental abnormality is a deviation from a norm, that we see it in its true light.

Clearly, this is not strictly a scientific or literary-critical problem. It is an ideological problem, deriving from the ontological dogma of the solitariness of man. The literature of realism, based on the Aristotelean concept of man as *zoon politikon*, is entitled to develop a new typology for each new phase in the evolution of a society. It displays the contradictions within society and within the individual in the context of a dialectical unity. Here, individuals embodying violent and extraordinary passions are still within the range of a socially normal typology (Shakespeare, Balzac, Stendhal). For, in this literature, the average man is simply a dimmer reflection of the contradictions always existing in man and society; eccentricity is a socially-conditioned distortion. Obviously, the passions of the great heroes must not be confused with 'eccentricity' in the colloquial sense: Christian Buddenbrook is an 'eccentric'; Adrian Leverkühn is not.

The ontology of *Geworfenheit* makes a true typology impossible; it is replaced by an abstract polarity of the eccentric and the socially-average. We have seen why this polarity—which in traditional realism serves to increase our understanding of social normality—leads in modernism to a fascination with morbid eccentricity. Eccentricity becomes the necessary complement of the average; and this polarity is held to exhaust human potentiality. The implications of this ideology are shown in another remark of Musil's: 'If humanity dreamt collectively, it would dream Moosbrugger.' Moosbrugger, you will remember, was a mentally-retarded sexual pervert with homicidal tendencies.

What served, with Musil, as the ideological basis of a new typology—escape into neurosis as a protest against the evils of society—becomes with other modernist writers an immutable *condition humaine*. Musil's statement loses its conditional 'if' and becomes a simple description of reality. Lack of objectivity in the description of the outer world finds its complement in the reduction of reality to a nightmare. Beckett's *Molloy* is perhaps the *ne plus ultra* of this development, although Joyce's vision of reality as an incoherent stream of consciousness had already assumed in Faulkner a nightmare quality. In Beckett's novel we have the same vision twice over. He presents us with an image of the utmost human degradation—an idiot's vegetative existence. Then, as help is imminent from a mysterious unspecified source,

31

the rescuer himself sinks into idiocy. The story is told through the parallel streams of consciousness of the idiot and of his rescuer.

Along with the adoption of perversity and idiocy as types of the *condition humaine*, we find what amounts to frank glorification. Take Montherlant's *Pasiphae*, where sexual perversity—the heroine's infatuation with a bull—is presented as a triumphant return to nature, as the liberation of impulse from the slavery of convention. The chorus—i.e. the author—puts the following question (which, though rhetorical, clearly expects an affirmative reply): 'Si l'absence de pensée et l'absence de morale ne contribuent pas beaucoup à la dignité des bêtes, des plantes et des eaux ... ?' Montherlant expresses as plainly as Musil, though with different moral and emotional emphasis, the hidden —one might say repressed—social character of the protest underlying this obsession with psychopathology, its perverted Rousseauism, its anarchism. There are many illustrations of this in modernist writing. A poem of Benn's will serve to make the point:

> O that we were our primal ancestors,
> Small lumps of plasma in hot, sultry swamps;
> Life, death, conception, parturition
> Emerging from those juices soundlessly.
>
> A frond of seaweed or a dune of sand,
> Formed by the wind and heavy at the base;
> A dragonfly or gull's wing—already, these
> Would signify excessive suffering.

This is not overtly perverse in the manner of Beckett or Montherlant. Yet, in his primitivism, Benn is at one with them. The opposition of man as animal to man as social being (for instance, Heidegger's devaluation of the social as 'das Man', Klages' assertion of the incompatibility of *Geist* and *Seele*, or Rosenberg's racial mythology) leads straight to a glorification of the abnormal and to an undisguised anti-humanism.

A typology limited in this way to the *homme moyen sensuel* and the idiot also opens the door to 'experimental' stylistic distortion. Distortion becomes as inseparable a part of the portrayal of reality as the recourse to the pathological. But literature must have a concept of the normal if it is to 'place' distortion correctly; that is to say, to see it *as* distortion. With such a typology this placing is impossible, since the normal is no longer a proper object of literary interest. Life under capitalism is, often rightly, presented as a distortion (a petrification or paralysis) of the human substance. But to present psychopathology as a way of escape from this distortion is itself a distortion. We are invited to measure one type of distortion against another and arrive, necessarily, at universal distortion. There is no principle to set against the general pattern, no standard by which the petty-bourgeois and the pathological can be seen in their social context. And these tendencies, far from being relativized with time, become ever more absolute. Distortion becomes the normal condition of human existence; the proper study, the formative principle, of art and literature.

I have demonstrated some of the literary implications of this ideology. Let us now pursue the argument further. It is clear, I think, that modernism must deprive literature of a sense of *perspective*. This would not be surprising; rigorous modernists such as Kafka, Benn, and Musil have always indignantly refused to provide their readers with any such thing. I will return to the ideological implications of the idea of perspective later. Let me say here that, in any work of art, perspective is of overriding importance. It determines the course and content; it draws together the threads of the narration; it enables the artist to choose between the important and the superficial, the crucial and the episodic. The direction in which characters develop is determined by perspective, only those features being described which are material to their development. The more lucid the perspective— as in Molière or the Greeks—the more economical and striking the selection.

Modernism drops this selective principle. It asserts that it can dispense with it, or can replace it with its dogma of the *condition humaine*. A naturalistic style is bound to be the result. This state of affairs—which to my mind characterizes all modernist art of the past fifty years—is disguised by critics who systematically glorify the modernist movement. By concentrating on formal criteria, by isolating technique from content and exaggerating its importance, these critics refrain from judgment on the social or artistic significance of subject-matter. They are unable, in consequence, to make the aesthetic distinction between *realism* and *naturalism*. This distinction depends on the presence or absence in a work of art of a 'hierarchy of significance' in the situations and characters presented. Compared with this, formal categories are of secondary importance. That is why it is possible to speak of the basically *naturalistic* character of modernist literature—and to see here the literary expression of an ideological continuity. This is not to deny that variations in style reflect changes in society. But the particular form this principle of naturalistic arbitrariness, this lack of hierarchic structure, may take is not decisive. We encounter it in the all-determining 'social conditions' of Naturalism, in Symbolism's impressionist methods and its cultivation of the exotic, in the fragmentation of objective reality in Futurism and Constructivism and the German *Neue Sachlichkeit*, or, again, in Surrealism's stream of consciousness.

These schools have in common a basically static approach to reality. This is closely related to their lack of perspective. Characteristically, Gottfried Benn actually incorporated this in his artistic programme. One of his volumes bears the title, *Static Poems*. The denial of history, of development, and thus of perspective, becomes the mark of true insight into the nature of reality.

> The wise man is ignorant
> of change and development
> his children and children's children
> are no part of his world.

The rejection of any concept of the future is for Benn the criterion of wisdom. But even those modernist writers who are less extreme in their rejection of history tend to present social and historical phenomena as static. It is, then, of small importance whether this condition is 'eternal', or only a transitional stage punctuated by sudden catastrophes (even in early Naturalism the static presentation was often broken up by these catastrophes, without altering its basic character). Musil, for instance, writes in his essay, *The Writer in our Age*: 'One knows just as little about the present. Partly, this is because we are, as always, too close to the present. But it is also because the present into which we were plunged some two decades ago is of a particularly all-embracing and inescapable character.' Whether or not Musil knew of Heidegger's philosophy, the idea of *Geworfenheit* is clearly at work here. And the following reveals plainly how, for Musil, this static state was upset by the catastrophe of 1914: 'All of a sudden, the world was full of violence. . . . In European civilization, there was a sudden rift. . . .' In short: thus static apprehension of reality in modernist literature is no passing fashion; it is rooted in the ideology of modernism.

To establish the basic distinction between modernism and that realism which, from Homer to Thomas Mann and Gorky, has assumed change and development to be the proper subject of literature, we must go deeper into the underlying ideological problem. In *The House of the Dead* Dostoevsky gave an interesting account of the convict's attitude to work. He described how the prisoners, in spite of brutal discipline, loafed about, working badly or merely going through the motions of work until a new overseer arrived and allotted them a new project, after which they were allowed to go home. 'The work was hard,' Dostoevsky continues, 'but, Christ, with what energy they threw themselves into it! Gone was all their former indolence and pretended incompetence.' Later in the book Dostoevsky sums up his experiences: 'If a man loses hope and has no aim in view, sheer boredom can turn him into a beast. . . .' I have said that the problem of perspective in literature is directly related to the principle of selection. Let me go further: underlying the problem is a profound ethical complex, reflected in the composition of the work itself. Every human action is based on a presupposition of its inherent meaningfulness, at least to the subject. Absence of meaning makes a mockery of action and reduces art to naturalistic description.

Clearly, there can be no literature without at least the appearance of change or development. This conclusion should not be interpreted in a narrowly metaphysical sense. We have already diagnosed the obsession with psychopathology in modernist literature as a desire to escape from the reality of capitalism. But this implies the absolute primacy of the *terminus a quo*, the condition from which it is desired to escape. Any movement towards a *terminus ad quem* is condemned to impotence. As the ideology of most modernist writers asserts the unalterability of outward reality (even if this is reduced to a mere state of consciousness) human activity is, *a priori*, rendered impotent and robbed of meaning.

The apprehension of reality to which this leads is most consistently and convincingly realized in the work of Kafka. Kafka remarks of Josef K., as he is being led to execution: 'He thought of flies, their tiny limbs breaking as they struggle away from the fly-paper.' This mood of total impotence, of paralysis in the face of the unintelligible power of circumstances, informs all his work. Though the action of *The Castle* takes a different, even an opposite, direction to that of *The Trial*, this view of the world, from the perspective of a trapped and struggling fly, is all-pervasive. This experience, this vision of a world dominated by *angst* and of man at the mercy of incomprehensible terrors, makes Kafka's work the very type of modernist art. Techniques, elsewhere of merely formal significance, are used here to evoke a primitive awe in the presence of an utterly strange and hostile reality. Kafka's *angst* is the experience *par excellence* of modernism.

Two instances from musical criticism—which can afford to be both franker and more theoretical than literary criticism—

show that it is indeed a universal experience with which we are dealing. The composer, Hanns Eisler, says of Schönberg: 'Long before the invention of the bomber, he expressed what people were to feel in the air raid shelters.' Even more characteristic— though seen from a modernist point of view—is Theodor W. Adorno's analysis (in *The Ageing of Modern Music*) of symptoms of decadence in modernist music: 'The sounds are still the same. But the experience of *angst*, which made their originals great, has vanished.' Modernist music, he continues, has lost touch with the truth that was its *raison d'être*. Composers are no longer equal to the emotional presuppositions of their modernism. And that is why modernist music has failed. The diminution of the original *angst*-obsessed vision of life (whether due, as Adorno thinks, to inability to respond to the magnitude of the horror or, as I believe, to the fact that this obsession with *angst* among bourgeois intellectuals has already begun to recede) has brought about a loss of substance in modern music, and destroyed its authenticity as a modernist art-form.

This is a shrewd analysis of the paradoxical situation of the modernist artist, particularly where he is trying to express deep and genuine experience. The deeper the experience, the greater the damage to the artistic whole. But this tendency towards disintegration, this loss of artistic unity, cannot be written off as a mere fashion, the product of experimental gimmicks. Modern philosophy, after all, encountered these problems long before modern literature, painting or music. A case in point is the problem of *time*. Subjective Idealism had already separated time, abstractly conceived, from historical change and particularity of place. As if this separation were insufficient for the new age of imperialism, Bergson widened it further. Experienced time, subjective time, now became identical with real time; the rift between this time and that of the objective world was complete. Bergson and other philosophers who took up and varied this theme claimed that their concept of time alone afforded insight into authentic, i.e. subjective, reality. The same tendency soon made its appearance in literature.

The German left-wing critic and essayist of the Twenties, Walter Benjamin, has well described Proust's vision and the techniques he uses to present it in his great novel: 'We all know that Proust does not describe a man's life as it actually happens, but as it is remembered by a man who has lived through it. Yet this puts it far too crudely. For it is not actual experience that is important, but the texture of reminiscence, the Penelope's tapestry of a man's memory.' The connection with Bergson's theories of time is obvious. But whereas with Bergson, in the abstraction of philosophy, the unity of perception is preserved, Benjamin shows that with Proust, as a result of the radical disintegration of the time sequence, objectivity is eliminated: 'A lived event is finite, concluded at least on the level of experience. But a remembered event is infinite, a possible key to everything that preceded it and to everything that will follow it.'

It is the distinction between a philosophical and an artistic vision of the world. However hard philosophy, under the influence of Idealism, tries to liberate the concepts of space and time from temporal and spatial particularity, literature continues to assume their unity. The fact that, nevertheless, the concept of subjective time cropped up in literature only shows how deeply subjectivism is rooted in the experience of the modern bourgeois intellectual. The individual, retreating into himself in despair at the cruelty of the age, may experience an intoxicated fascination with his forlorn condition. But then a new horror breaks through. If reality cannot be understood (or no effort is made to understand it), then the individual's subjectivity—alone in the universe, reflecting only itself—takes on an equally incomprehensible and horrific character. Hugo von Hofmannsthal was to experience this condition very early in his poetic career:

> It is a thing that no man cares to think on,
> And far too terrible for mere complaint,
> That all things slip from us and pass away,
>
> And that my ego, bound by no outward force—
> Once a small child's before it became mine—
> Should now be strange to me, like a strange dog.

By separating time from the outer world of objective reality, the inner world of the subject is transformed into a sinister, inexplicable flux and acquires—paradoxically, as it may seem—a static character.

On literature this tendency towards disintegration, of course, will have an even greater impact than on philosophy. When time is isolated in this way, the artist's world disintegrates into a multiplicity of partial worlds. The static view of the world, now combined with diminished objectivity, here rules unchallenged. The world of man—the only subject-matter of literature—is shattered if a single component is removed. I have shown the consequences of isolating time and reducing it to a subjective category. But time is by no means the only component whose removal can lead to such disintegration. Here, again, Hofmannsthal anticipated later developments. His imaginary 'Lord Chandos' reflects: 'I have lost the ability to concentrate my thoughts or set them out coherently.' The result is a condition of apathy, punctuated by manic fits. The development towards a definitely pathological protest is here anticipated—admittedly in glamorous, romantic guise. But it is the same disintegration that is at work.

Previous realistic literature, however violent its criticism of reality, had always assumed the unity of the world it described and seen it as a living whole inseparable from man himself. But the major realists of our time deliberately introduce elements of disintegration into their work—for instance, the subjectivizing of time—and use them to portray the contemporary world more exactly. In this way, the once natural unity becomes a conscious, constructed unity (I have shown elsewhere that the device of the two temporal planes in Thomas Mann's *Doctor Faustus* serves to emphasize its historicity). But in modernist literature the disintegration of the world of man—and consequently the disintegration of personality—coincides with the ideological intention. Thus *angst*, this basic modern experience, this by-product of *Geworfenheit*, has its emotional origin in the experience of a disintegrating society. But it attains its effects by evoking the disintegration of the world of man.

To complete our examination of modernist literature, we must consider for a moment the question of allegory. Allegory is that aesthetic genre which lends itself par excellence to a description of man's alienation from objective reality. Allegory is a problematic genre because it rejects that assumption of an immanent meaning to human existence which—however unconscious, however combined with religious concepts of transcendence—is the basis of traditional art. Thus in medieval art we observe a new secularity (in spite of the continued use of religious subjects) triumphing more and more, from the time of Giotto, over the allegorizing of an earlier period.

Certain reservations should be made at this point. First, we must distinguish between literature and the visual arts. In the latter, the limitations of allegory can be the more easily overcome in that transcendental, allegorical subjects can be clothed in an aesthetic immanence (even if of a merely decorative kind) and the rift in reality in some sense be eliminated—we have only to think of Byzantine mosaic art. This decorative element has no real equivalent in literature; it exists only in a figurative sense, and then only as a secondary component. Allegorical art of the quality of Byzantine mosaic is only rarely possible in literature. Secondly, we must bear in mind in examining allegory—and this is of great importance for our argument—a historical distinction: does the concept of transcendence in question contain within itself tendencies towards immanence (as in Byzantine art or Giotto), or is it the product precisely of a rejection of these tendencies?

Allegory, in modernist literature, is clearly of the latter kind. Transcendence implies here, more or less consciously, the negation of any meaning immanent in the world or the life of man. We have already examined the underlying ideological basis of this view and its stylistic consequences. To conclude our analysis, and to establish the allegorical character of modernist literature, I must refer again to the work of one of the finest theoreticians of modernism—to Walter Benjamin. Benjamin's examination of allegory was a product of his researches into German Baroque drama. Benjamin made his analysis of these relatively minor plays the occasion for a general discussion of the aesthetics of allegory. He was asking, in effect, why it is that transcendence, which is the essence of allegory, cannot but destroy aesthetics itself.

Benjamin gives a very contemporary definition of allegory. He does not labour the analogies between modern art and the Baroque (such analogies are tenuous at best, and were much overdone by the fashionable criticism of the time). Rather, he uses the Baroque drama to criticize modernism, imputing the characteristics of the latter to the former. In so doing, Benjamin became the first critic to attempt a philosophical analysis of the aesthetic paradox underlying modernist art. He writes:

> In Allegory, the *facies hippocratica* of history looks to the observer like a petrified primeval landscape. History, all the suffering and failure it contains, finds expression in the human face—or, rather, in the human skull. No sense of freedom, no classical proportion, no human emotion lives in its features—not only human existence in general, but the fate of every individual human being is symbolized in this most palpable token of mortality. This is the core of the allegorical vision, of the Baroque idea of history as the passion of the world; History is significant only in the stations of its corruption. Significance is a function of mortality—because it is death that marks the passage from corruptibility to meaningfulness.

Benjamin returns again and again to this link between allegory and the annihilation of history:

> In the light of this vision history appears, not as the gradual realization of the eternal, but as a process of inevitable decay. Allegory thus goes beyond beauty. What ruins are in the physical world, allegories are in the world of the mind.

Benjamin points here to the aesthetic consequences of modernism —though projected into the Baroque drama—more shrewdly and consistently than any of his contemporaries. He sees that the notion of objective time is essential to any understanding of history, and that the notion of subjective time is a product of a period of decline. 'A thorough knowledge of the problematic nature of art' thus becomes for him—correctly, from his point of view—one of the hall-marks of allegory in Baroque drama. It is problematic, on the one hand, because it is an art intent on expressing absolute transcendence that fails to do so because of the means at its disposal. It is also problematic because it is an art reflecting the corruption of the world and bringing about its own dissolution in the process. Benjamin discovers 'an immense, anti-aesthetic subjectivity' in Baroque literature, associated with 'a theologically-determined subjectivity'. (We shall presently show—a point I have discussed elsewhere in relation to Heidegger's philosophy—how in literature a 'religious atheism' of this kind can acquire a theological character.) Romantic— and, on a higher plane, Baroque—writers were well aware of this problem, and gave their understanding, not only theoretical, but artistic—that is to say allegorical—expression. 'The image,' Benjamin remarks, 'becomes a rune in the sphere of allegorical intuition. When touched by the light of theology, its symbolic beauty is gone. The false appearance of totality vanishes. The image dies; the parable no longer holds true; the world it once contained disappears.'

The consequences for art are far-reaching, and Benjamin does not hesitate to point them out: 'Every person, every object, every relationship can stand for something else. This transferability constitutes a devastating, though just, judgment on the profane world—which is thereby branded as a world where such things are of small importance.' Benjamin knows, of course, that although details are 'transferable', and thus insignificant, they are not banished from art altogether. On the contrary. Precisely in modern art, with which he is ultimately concerned, descriptive detail is often of an extraordinary sensuous, suggestive power— we think again of Kafka. But this, as we showed in the case of Musil (a writer who does not consciously aim at allegory) does not prevent the materiality of the world from undergoing permanent alteration, from becoming transferable and arbitrary. Just this, modernist writers maintain, is typical of their own apprehension of reality. Yet presented in this way, the world becomes, as Benjamin puts it, 'exalted and depreciated at the same time'. For the conviction that phenomena are *not* ultimately transferable is rooted in a belief in the world's rationality and in man's ability to penetrate its secrets. In realistic literature each descriptive detail is both *individual* and *typical*. Modern allegory, and modernist ideology, however, deny the *typical*. By destroying the coherence of the world, they reduce detail to the level of mere particularity (once again, the connection between modernism and naturalism is plain). Detail, in its allegorical transferability, though brought into a direct, if paradoxical connection with transcendence, becomes an abstract function of the transcendence to which it points. Modernist literature thus replaces concrete typicality with abstract particularity.

We are here applying Benjamin's paradox directly to aesthetics and criticism, and particularly to the aesthetics of modernism. And, though we have reversed his scale of values, we have not deviated from the course of his argument. Elsewhere, he speaks out even more plainly—as though the Baroque mask had fallen, revealing the modernist skull underneath :

> Allegory is left empty-handed. The forces of evil, lurking in its depths, owe their very existence to allegory. Evil is, precisely, the non-existence of that which allegory purports to represent.

The paradox Benjamin arrives at—his investigation of the aesthetics of Baroque tragedy has culminated in a negation of aesthetics—sheds a good deal of light on modernist literature, and particularly on Kafka. In interpreting his writings allegorically I am not, of course, following Max Brod, who finds a specifically religious allegory in Kafka's works. Kafka refuted any such interpretation in a remark he is said to have made to Brod himself : 'We are nihilistic figments, all of us; suicidal notions forming in God's mind.' Kafka rejected, too, the gnostic concept of

God as an evil demiurge: 'The world is a cruel whim of God, an evil day's work.' When Brod attempted to give this an optimistic slant, Kafka shrugged off the attempt ironically: 'Oh, hope enough, hope without end—but not, alas, for us.' These remarks, quoted by Benjamin in his brilliant essay on Kafka, point to the general spiritual climate of his work: 'His profoundest experience is of the hopelessness, the utter meaninglessness of man's world, and particularly that of present-day bourgeois man.' Kafka, whether he says so openly or not, is an atheist. An atheist, though, of that modern species who regard God's removal from the scene not as a liberation—as did Epicurus and the Encyclopedists—but as a token of the 'God-forsakenness' of the world, its utter desolation and futility. Jacobsen's *Niels Lyhne* was the first novel to describe this state of mind of the atheistic bourgeois intelligentsia. Modern religious atheism is characterized, on the one hand, by the fact that unbelief has lost its revolutionary *élan*—the empty heavens are the projection of a world beyond hope of redemption. On the other hand, religious atheism shows that the desire for salvation lives on with undiminished force in a world without God, worshipping the void created by God's absence.

The supreme judges in *The Trial*, the castle administration in *The Castle*, represent transcendence in Kafka's allegories: the transcendence of Nothingness. Everything points to them, and they could give meaning to everything. Everybody believes in their existence and omnipotence; but nobody knows them, nobody knows how they can be reached. If there is a God here, it can only be the God of religious atheism: *atheos absconditus*. We become acquainted with a repellent host of subordinate authorities; brutal, corrupt, pedantic—and, at the same time, unreliable and irresponsible. It is a portrait of the bourgeois society Kafka knew, with a dash of Prague local colouring. But it is also allegorical in that the doings of this bureaucracy and of those dependent on it, its impotent victims, are not concrete and realistic, but a reflection of that Nothingness which governs existence. The hidden, non-existent God of Kafka's world derives his spectral character from the fact that his own non-existence is the ground of all existence; and the portrayed reality, uncannily accurate as it is, is spectral in the shadow of that dependence. The only purpose of transcendence—the intangible *nichtendes Nichts*—is to reveal the *facies hippocratica* of the world.

That abstract particularity which we saw to be the aesthetic consequence of allegory reaches its high mark in Kafka. He is a marvellous observer; the spectral character of reality affects him so deeply that the simplest episodes have an oppressive, nightmarish immediacy. As an artist, he is not content to evoke the surface of life. He is aware that individual detail must point to general significance. But how does he go about the business of abstraction? He has emptied everyday life of meaning by using the allegorical method; he has allowed detail to be annihilated by his transcendental Nothingness. This allegorical transcendence bars Kafka's way to realism, prevents him from investing observed detail with typical significance. Kafka is not able, in spite of his extraordinary evocative power, in spite of his unique sensibility, to achieve that fusion of the particular and the general which is the essence of realistic art. His aim is to raise the individual detail in its immediate particularity (without generalizing its content) to the level of abstraction. Kafka's method is typical, here, of modernism's allegorical approach. Specific subject-matter and stylistic variation do not matter; what matters is the basic ideological determination of form and content. The particularity we find in Beckett and Joyce, in Musil and Benn, various as the treatment of it may be, is essentially of the same kind.

If we combine what we have up to now discussed separately we arrive at a consistent pattern. We see that modernism leads not only to the destruction of traditional literary forms; it leads to the destruction of literature as such. And this is true not only of Joyce, or of the literature of Expressionism and Surrealism. It was not André Gide's ambition, for instance, to bring about a revolution in literary style; it was his philosophy that compelled him to abandon conventional forms. He planned his *Faux-*

Monnayeurs as a novel. But its structure suffered from a characteristically modernist schizophrenia: it was supposed to be written by the man who was also the hero of the novel. And, in practice, Gide was forced to admit that no novel, no work of literature could be constructed in that way. We have here a practical demonstration that—as Benjamin showed in another context—modernism means not the enrichment, but the negation of art.

Franz Kafka or Thomas Mann?

TO DEFINE the conditions in which bourgeois 'literary' literature can flourish today, we analysed the ideological basis and the main stylistic tendencies of the modern bourgeois anti-realistic movement. We might have widened our examination to include 'non-literary' literature, if only to reveal its social basis. Certain of the phenomena we have discussed are to be found most strikingly in this latter literature. Take the cult of the abnormal, of the perverse: horror comics show that this cult is drawn directly from life. Or take the detective story. With Conan Doyle the genre was firmly grounded in a philosophy of security; it glorified the omniscience of those who watched over the stability of bourgeois life. Now the basic ingredients are fear and insecurity: at any moment terror may break through; only luck can avert it. In some works of a middle-brow kind (for example in Hayes' *On a day like any other*) this kind of 'luck' provides—by way of apology for the society it portrays—the book's happy ending. Indeed, a main distinction between highbrow literature and the literature of entertainment is just this rejection of a compromise—though there is a modern variety of the thriller which deliberately exploits horror for its own purposes.

But we must return to our proper subject: to modernism, or rather to those modernist techniques so influential on the contemporary literary scene. We avoided the use of purely formal criteria in distinguishing between modernist and realist literature. Yet ideological criteria, though they underlie and mould literary expression, also represent no more than general tendencies. These may co-exist in one author, even in one work of art, with varying degrees of emphasis and self-consciousness.

Indeed, if we refuse to follow those modernist critics who tell us that theirs is the only possible future literature, and trace the realist tendencies still existing within the anti-realistic movement, the literature of our time begins to resemble an extended battlefield. It is a battlefield where the champions of modern anti-realism, and the champions of what we have called 'the revolt of humanism', noisily contend. What we are examining is not simply two typical literary movements of our time. We are examining a conflict between two basic tendencies, a conflict fought out, not only in one and the same writer, but often in one and the same poem, play, or novel.

The dividing line is often blurred, if only because all writing must contain a certain degree of realism. Indeed, there is a fundamental truth at stake here: realism is not one style among others, it is the basis of literature; all styles (even those seemingly most opposed to realism) originate in it or are significantly related to it. Schopenhauer's remark that a consistent solipsist could only be found in a lunatic asylum is applicable to consistent anti-realism. The inevitability of realism is most obvious, of course, where descriptive detail is concerned. We have only to think of Kafka, where the most improbable, fantastic statements appear real through force of descriptive detail. Without this realism in detail Kafka's evocation of the spectral nature of human existence would be no more than a sermon, not the inexorable nightmare it is. Realistic detail is a precondition for the communication of a sense of absurdity. We get, in fact, not straightforward anti-realism, but a dialectical process in which realism of detail negates the reality described; everything is determined by it—the presentation, the structure, the coherence of the writing. Similar processes are at work elsewhere in other modernist literature. But the tension Kafka achieves by pushing his two poles to their extremes, and by the shock of his transitions, is lacking. In Musil, too, we find this tension, but it owes less to intensity of detail and is spread out over the whole extent of his novel. We encounter dialectical leaps from 'documentary' (with regard to some of the characters the novel is a *roman à*

48

clef) to intimations of timelessness—attempts to achieve that 'ahistoric', 'paradigmatic' ambience which Musil claimed for the work.

Of still greater importance is the fact that many—and not the least extreme—components of modernist literature (for instance, the problem of time) are not as far removed from contemporary life as it might seem. On the contrary, they reflect very well certain aspects of reality, certain contemporary characteristics and peculiarities (of a certain social class, at least). Even with the most abstruse anti-realistic writers, stylistic experiment is not the wilful twisting of reality according to subjective whim: it is a consequence of conditions prevailing in the modern world. Modernist forms, like other literary forms, reflect social and historical realities—though in a distorted, and distorting, fashion.

The situation is immensely complicated; it is natural that in the private statements and public manifestoes of leading modernist writers the issues are often blurred. It is not enough to point to the protests against the suppression of 'degenerate art' under Hitler. These protests proclaimed general freedom of literary expression, but they defended more specifically the writer's duty to describe reality as his artistic conscience dictates. Since truth was the enemy of Hitlerism, a protest against its persecution of 'degenerate art' was at the same time a defence of realism.

The motives of the modernists' opposition to Stalinist dogmatism's rejection of 'formalism' are likewise mixed. Defence of extreme modernism (including genuinely 'formalistic' literature) goes hand in hand with a—justified—rejection of the dogmatists' over-simplifications about the subject-matter and style of realism, and of their tendency to suppress the contradictions existing in socialist society, their reduction of 'socialist perspective' to childish 'happy endings'.

Attacks of this kind may cause the pendulum to swing to the other extreme. Seeing that dogmatism paralyses originality, the modernist critic is tempted to contrast—an understandable, though objectively incorrect reaction—the 'interesting' colourfulness of decadent art with the 'greyness' of schematic social-realist pseudo-literature. In the process he is likely to dismiss the theory of socialist realism as an obstacle to artistic freedom. The significant aesthetic antagonism between realism and anti-realism is no longer considered worth discussing; the merits of socialist (and critical) realism are disregarded; and the deeply problematical nature of modernism itself is ignored. In this context, it is worth pointing out the schematism of so many of the most highly praised creations of modernism. Formal novelty, and an affected originality, often conceal a subjectivist dogmatism. Ernst Jünger and Gottfried Benn, James Joyce and Samuel Beckett are not, properly speaking, a whit less schematic than many social-realist writers.

More significant than such polemics—where often enough the adversary, rather than the object to be defended, seems to determine the course of the argument—are the utterances of those critical realists who had an interest in, and concern for, the formal experimentation of modernism, and expressed the conviction that they had many basic attitudes in common. The reason is not far to seek. Many of these experiments are, in effect, reflections of contemporary reality. If realistic writers sympathize with these experiments, and are stimulated thereby to widen the scope of realism, it is because they wish to find new means to deal with contemporary subject-matter. We have only to think of Thomas Mann's published opinions of Kafka, Joyce, or Gide.

However blurred in a particular work of art, these distinctions exist; and can often be traced in individual cases with some precision. They are, indeed, more than bare distinctions; they are often mutually exclusive contradictions. We have already pointed to examples of polarization of content and, as a consequence, of form in cases that appear superficially similar—the handling of the stream-of-consciousness technique in Joyce and Thomas Mann, and the apparently similar, though in fact diametrically opposed, treatment of time. And there is a reason for this outward convergence in spite of extreme inner divergence. While the modernist writer is uncritical towards many aspects of the modern world, his contemporary, the realist writer, can step back from these things and treat them with the necessary critical detachment. To take the problem of time: Thomas Mann's critical detachment is such that he is not in doubt about the subjective character of the modern experience of time. Yet he knows that this experience is typical only of a certain social class, which can best be portrayed by making use of this experience. The uncritical approach of modernist writers—and of some modern philosophers—reveals itself in their conviction that this subjective experience constitutes reality as such. That is why this treatment of time can be used by the realistic writer to characterize certain figures in his novels, although in a modernist work it may be used to describe reality itself. Again and again Thomas Mann places characters with a time-experience of this subjectivist kind in relation to characters whose experience of time is normal and objective. In *The Magic Mountain* Hans Castorp represents the former type; Joachim Ziemssen and Hofrat Behrens the latter. Ziemssen is aware that this experience of time may be a result of living in a sanatorium, hermetically sealed off from everyday life. We arrive, therefore, at an important distinction: the modernist writer identifies what is necessarily a subjective experience with reality as such, thus giving a distorted picture of reality as a whole (Virginia Woolf is an extreme example of this). The realist, with his critical detachment, places what is a significant, specifically modern experience in a wider context, giving it only the emphasis it deserves as part of a greater, objective whole.

The same distinction is valid with regard to descriptive detail. In isolation, descriptive detail may be a genuine enough reflection of reality—that is, if the writer in question has talent. But whether or not the sequence and organization make for an adequate image of objective reality will depend on the writer's attitude towards reality as a whole. For this attitude determines the function which the individual detail is accorded in the context of the whole. If it is handled uncritically, the result may be an arbitrary naturalism, since the writer will not be able to distinguish between significant and irrelevant detail. Joyce, I think, is a case in point. Once again, the essentially *naturalistic* character of modernism comes to the fore.

The matter becomes more complex with Kafka. Kafka is one of the very few modernist writers whose attitude to detail is selective, not naturalistic. Formally, his treatment of detail is not dissimilar to that of a realist. The difference becomes apparent only when we examine his basic commitment, the principles determining the selection and sequence of detail. With Kafka these principles are his belief in a transcendental force (Nothingness); in his nihilistic allegories, therefore, the artistic unity is broken.

But the problem cannot be approached formalistically. There are great realistic writers in whose work immediate social and historical reality is transcended, where realism in detail is based on a belief in a supernatural world. Take E. T. A. Hoffmann, for example. In Hoffmann, realism in detail goes hand in hand with a belief in the spectral nature of reality. On closer inspection, though, the difference between his artistic aims and those of modernism is apparent. Hoffmann's world is—for all its fairy-tale, ghostly ambience—an accurate enough reflection of conditions in the Germany of his time, a country moving from a distorted feudal absolutism to a capitalism not less distorted. With Hoffmann the supernatural was a means of presenting the German situation in its totality, at a time when social conditions did not as yet allow a direct realistic description or, indeed, as yet reveal a typical pattern. The working out of a typology was much easier in more highly developed France—though even Balzac at times used methods developed by Hoffmann (*Melmoth Reconcilié*).

Kafka is more secular than Hoffmann. His ghosts belong to everyday bourgeois life; and, since this life itself is unreal, there is no need of supernatural ghosts à la Hoffmann. But the unity of the world is broken up, since an essentially subjective vision is identified with reality itself. The terror generated by the world of imperialist capitalism (anticipatory of its later fascist progeny), where human beings are degraded to mere objects—this fear, originally a subjective experience, becomes an objective entity.

The reflection of a distortion becomes a distorted reflection. And though Kafka's artistic method differs from that of other modernist writers, the principle of presentation is the same: the world is an allegory of transcendent Nothingness. With Kafka's followers the differences grow smaller or disappear altogether. With Beckett, for example, who mixes Kafkaesque and Joycean motifs, a fully standardized nihilistic modernism is the end-product.

In rejecting a rigid distinction, and acknowledging that in many cases the distinction is blurred, I must not be taken to imply that no real opposition exists. On the contrary, only by this method can the conflict of tendencies be accurately assessed. To sum up our enquiry so far: similarity of technique does not imply similarity of ideology; nor is the approval or rejection of certain techniques a pointer to a writer's basic aim.

But what is this basic aim? So far, we have dealt with the main components of modernism, tracing the central ideological position common to its various schools. In order to establish our distinction we must return to the question of *perspective*. First, we must show how perspective acts as a principle of selection, as the criterion by which a writer selects his detail and avoids the pitfalls of naturalism. Clearly, this problem faces every talented writer: literary talent implies an affection for the richness and diversity of life. How the individual writer imposes some kind of order on the profusion of sensuous impression is chiefly a biographical question. These two dialectically opposed, yet dialectically complementary, activities are basic to the formation of an individual style. And here the importance of perspective as the selective principle must be evident. Max Liebermann, the Berlin Impressionist, used to say: 'To draw is to subtract.' We might extend that aphorism: art is the selection of the essential and subtraction of the inessential.

In itself, this is too abstract a definition. If it is to be of practical use, we must enquire more deeply into the subjective principle guiding artistic selection, and investigate the convergence (or divergence) between the data selected by an individual writer and 'artistic objectivity'. The latter is clearly not a direct consequence of the former; the degree of sincerity, intensity and insight guiding artistic selection is no guarantee, let alone a criterion, of objectivity. Yet it would be wrong to see the two principles as ineluctably opposed. Certainly, there is a divergence between subjective aim and objective achievement. But it is not something abrupt and irrational, a distinction between two metaphysical entities. Rather, it is part of the dialectical process by which a creative subjectivity develops, and is expressive of that subjectivity's encounter with the world of its time (or, possibly, of its failure to come to terms with that world).

A writer's pattern of choice is a function of his personality. But personality is not in fact timeless and absolute, however it may appear to the individual consciousness. Talent and character may be innate; but the manner in which they develop, or fail to develop, depends on the writer's interaction with his environment, on his relationships with other human beings. His life is part of the life of his time; no matter whether he is conscious of this, approves of it or disapproves. He is part of a larger social and historical whole.

His own life is thus never constant or static; it is a process, a running battle between past, present and future. It is something which cannot be measured or understood until its stages have been experienced as a movement from and towards a certain goal. These stages and their dynamic interrelations are not purely subjective elements, to be accepted or rejected by the writer at his discretion. Life itself, the categories determining its nature and development, would be distorted if such factors were to be arbitrarily eliminated.

Up to this point, and within the framework of this rather abstract philosophical analysis, I may have the reader's approval. But a historical phenomenon is historical not only in this general sense; it is also a *concrete* element in a specific historical process, in a concrete present linking a concrete past and future. It follows that everything in a writer's life, every individual experience, thought and emotion he undergoes, however subjective, partakes of a historical character. Every element in his life as a human being and as a writer is part of, and determined by, the movement from and towards some goal. Any authentic reflection of reality in literature must point to this movement. The method adopted will vary, of course, with the period and personality. But the selection and subtraction he undertakes in response to the teleological pattern of his own life constitutes the most intimate link between a writer's subjectivity and the outside world. We observe here a dialectical leap from the profound inwardness of subjectivity to the objectivity of social and historical reality.

In all this, *perspective* plays a decisive role. To understand its importance we must go into the distinction between objective reality and its artistic reflection rather more fully. It is a truism that the roots of the present are in the past, and the roots of the future in the present. Objectively, perspective points to the main movements in a given historical process. Subjectively—and not only in the field of artistic activity—it represents the capacity to grasp the existence and mode of action of these movements. If literature is to render an image of life that is adequate, formally convincing and consistent, the sequence must be reversed. Whereas in life 'whither?' is a consequence of 'whence?', in literature 'whither?' determines the content, selection and proportion of the various elements. The finished work may resemble life in observing a causal sequence; but it would be no more than an arbitrary chronicle if there were not this reversal of direction. It is the perspective, the *terminus ad quem*, that determines the significance of each element in a work of art.

The creative role of perspective goes even further than this and touches on the creative act itself. It is not enough, however, to demonstrate the general connection between perspective and literary creativity. The concreteness of a writer's perspective, of course, is a decisive influence on the vitality and suggestive power of his art. It is decisive in as much as there is a connection— not direct, but complex and devious—between the structure of individual character and the degree to which perspective, in a work of art, can be realized. An *aesthetic* explanation of this connection has never been attempted; nor, I think, has the question ever been posed. In this place, we can do no more than enquire into one or two extreme examples. And this only in relation to our specific problem—to discover what perspective is favourable to the development of critical realism at the present day.

The following points seem to me worth making. First, there exists a somewhat abstract perspective, which makes use of the general features of an historical period, and can be employed in satire to work out typical characters and situations (Swift, Saltykov-Shchedrin). Clearly, typical situations will be technically easier to realize than characters which are individual and typical at the same time. Secondly, at the opposite extreme, there is the kind of perspective mainly concerned with day-to-day depiction of events, and which encourages the naturalistic description of individual or superficially typical features. The dialectic of historical development is labyrinthine; and, especially in regard to individual particularities, is not open to detached contemporary prediction. Only 'prophetic' vision, or subsequent study of a completed period, can grasp the unity underlying sharp contradictions. One would be misunderstanding the role of perspective in literature, though, if one were to identify 'prophetic' understanding with correct political foresight. If such foresight were the criterion, there would have been no successful typology in nineteenth-century literature. For it was precisely the greatest writers of that age—Balzac and Stendhal, Dickens and Tolstoy— who erred most in their view of what the future would be like. Yet it was not accident that made possible the creation of typical, universal characters in their work.

Typology and perspective are thus related in a special way. The great realist writer is alone able to grasp and portray trends and phenomena truthfully in their historical development— 'trends' not so much in the social and political field, as in that area where human behaviour is moulded and evaluated, where existing types are developed further and new types emerge. Men are changed by forces in their environment. But it is not only the character of individual human beings that changes. Greater em-

FRANZ KAFKA OR THOMAS MANN?

phasis is given at certain times to certain specific problems: some
are pushed into the foreground, others eliminated; certain characteristics acquire a tragic aura, others, tragic in the past, are
now reduced to comic dimensions. Such shifts of emphasis go on
perpetually throughout history. Yet only the greatest realists
are equipped to understand and portray their complexity.

A writer may grasp the authentic human problem (and thus
the authentic social problem) of a particular phase in the historical process without consciously anticipating subsequent political
and social developments. Here again, the question of perspective
is relevant. For a typology can only be of lasting significance if
the writer has depicted the central or peripheral significance,
the comic or tragic characteristics of his types, in such a way
that subsequent developments confirm his portrait of the age.
(Balzac and Tolstoy have this kind of lasting significance; Ibsen,
by way of contrast, has dated in many respects). We see now
that perspective is not to be confused with the capacity to predict
historical events. Yet we also see why a perspective that sticks too
closely to day-to-day events is rarely successful: concrete and
determinate in matters which are of small interest to literature,
it fails to produce adequate aesthetic solutions in more important
matters. Lasting typologies, based on a perspective of this sort,
owe their effectiveness not to the artist's understanding of day-
to-day events, but to his unconscious possession of a perspective
independent of, and reaching beyond, his understanding of the
contemporary scene.

Perspective, in this concrete form, is central to our problem.
For there is an intimate connection between a writer's ability
to create lasting human types (the real criterion of literary
achievement) and his allegiance to an ideology which allows
of a belief in social development. Any attempt to substitute a
static immobilism for the dynamic movement of history must
reduce the significance, the universality, of the typology in question. Even in the Naturalist period the difficulty of creating living characters had increased so much that a writer of Zola's
stature could not create one really memorable character. The

state of affairs in modernist literature is still more striking. It takes, of course, a different form with each individual writer. But we are less interested in the particular form the reduction takes—whether the reduction of character to shadowy blur, or a submission to a rigid and superficial stylization, or a surrender to mystical irrationalism. Equally, there will be modernist theoreticians who refuse to admit that this reduction is anything negative. They will claim for Beckett's characters the dignity of a new typology, or reject the whole business of type-creation as a hangover from the nineteenth century.

It may be useful here to listen to the views of certain writers whose approach is not ideological and philosophical, but who are guided rather by practical experience of their craft. In a different context, some years ago, I quoted a remark of Sinclair Lewis' about John Dos Passos. Lewis praised Dos Passos' 'natural'—i.e. modernist—compositional methods as an enormous advance on older narrative conventions. Yet, speaking of the creation of character, he was forced to conclude: 'It is undeniable that Dos Passos has failed so far to produce characters as memorable as Pickwick, Micawber, Oliver Twist or David Copperfield or Nicholas Nickleby . . . and he will probably never do so.'

No less interesting is a confession of Camus's in his preface to the writings of Roger Martin du Gard. Martin du Gard's characters, Camus remarks, display a density, a three-dimensionality, very unusual in contemporary literature. The significant literature of our time, he continues, goes back to Dostoevsky rather than to Tolstoy. Its heroes are passionate, gesticulating shadows meditating upon human fate. Camus brilliantly contrasts Dostoevsky's young women in *The Possessed* with Tolstoy's Natasha Rostova: 'The distinction is like that between a film and stage character: the presence is spiritual, incorporeal.' I have no space here to comment on Camus's illuminating discussion of Dostoevsky and Kafka. The contrast between the two artistic modes is worked out with remarkable impartiality. Camus does not omit to point out that Dostoevsky's art is infinitely richer than that of his followers, who often inherit little more than the shadowiness to which he reduces human personality.

This judgment is the more interesting as we find in Camus's own work a comparable reduction of human personality. For, however suggestive as an allegory of the *condition humaine,* and however subtle the moral problems thrown up by Camus's description of the plague, the characters in *La Peste* remain, by Camus's definition, shadows. Yet it is not the spare style, maintained with marvellous consistency, which has brought about this reduction; it is the lack of perspective. The lives of his characters are without direction, without motivation, without development. Camus's plague—the choice of subject-matter is characteristic—is not shown as an accidental disaster, as a horrific interlude in the continuity of human life. The plague is the reality of human existence itself, the terror of which has no beginning and no end. Camus's admiration for Roger Martin du Gard's typology is significant, because it contains a profound, though unstated, criticism of his own work.

These apparent digressions may, I hope, have served to shed some light on the role of perspective in literature. We must now take a further, decisive step in the argument—with the proposition that no writer of the past century, asking himself to what goal history is moving, has been able to ignore socialism.

The writers of the 'humanist revolt', and their contemporaries, had to face this challenge. It was Zola who said that whenever he set out to tackle a new problem he always came up against socialism. Again, it is significant for Gerhart Hauptmann's artistic development—and for the enormous impact of his early Naturalist work—that the problem of socialism, though vaguely articulated, was always present in his mind. Once this vision lost its validity for him, Hauptmann plunged into that prolonged creative crisis which caused his admirers to fear for his future as a writer. There is no lack of other examples: the decisive role played by socialism in the work of Anatole France, of Romain Rolland, of George Bernard Shaw, is sufficiently well-known. And Roger Martin du Gard's criticism of bourgeois society, in his cycle of novels, is no less determined by a *terminus ad quem* of this kind—Jacques Thibault's encounter with socialism.

A simple conclusion would appear to be available at this point. Is not the decisive distinction that between the presence of a socialist perspective in socialist realism, and its absence in decadent bourgeois literature?

The conclusion is tempting, but false. For the distinction I have in mind, the ideological and artistic implications of which I am concerned to analyse, is operative within bourgeois literature itself. The true opposition is not between socialist realism and bourgeois modernism, but between bourgeois critical realism and bourgeois modernism. Not everyone who looks for a solution to the social and ideological crisis of bourgeois society—and this is necessarily the subject-matter of contemporary bourgeois literature—will be a professed socialist. It is enough that a writer takes socialism into account and does not reject it out of hand. But if he rejects socialism—and this is the point I want to make —he closes his eyes to the future, gives up any chance of assessing the present correctly, and loses the ability to create other than purely static works of art.

Ideologically, this question has been central to bourgeois literature throughout the past century; indeed, it has become increasingly urgent. Let us look at some of its earlier appearances. A hundred years ago Heine wrote in a preface to the French edition of *Lutezia* that communism, though it was against his interests and his natural inclinations, had an attraction he found hard to resist. One reason for this attraction was communism's emphasis on logic and on justice. The unjust society he lived in stood condemned—even though the new society, as he put it, should use his *Buch der Lieder* as 'wrapping paper for an old lady's coffee'. Another reason was as cogent, if Machiavellian: the communists were the most powerful enemies of his own old enemy, German reaction and German chauvinism. In spite of all this, Heine never became a socialist. But he did take up a position towards socialism which enabled him to look at the bourgeois society of his day, and at the future, without illusions.

Let us look at the changing forms perspective has taken for the bourgeois writer over the course of history. Before the French Revolution, realism did not have to face this problem. Perspective went no further than the overthrow of the feudal society of absolutism. The shape of the new bourgeois society was—from the point of view of the artist—of secondary importance. This was to change after the French Revolution. The degree to which the works of Goethe and Balzac, of Stendhal and Tolstoy, are still interlarded with utopian elements is very striking. It expresses their ambiguity towards bourgeois society. On the one hand, we still find a bourgeois-progressive perspective (with Tolstoy, it is still peasant-plebeian) which is rooted in, and does not look beyond, bourgeois society. But on the other hand there is a deeply felt need to go beyond the mere affirmation of existing conditions, to explore values not to be found in present society— values which come to be thought of, necessarily, as hidden in the future. Thus the utopian perspective serves a double function: it enables the artist to portray the present age truthfully without giving way to despair.

A later phase of critical realism—Flaubert is a good example— rejects such utopianism with a gesture of ascetic defiance. Utopian writing in this period takes the form of an escape into exoticisms whether of time or place. This dual critique—ironic detachment from his own ineradicable romanticism, but also rejection of a bourgeois world condemned by the standards of that romanticism—enabled Flaubert to view his age without hope, but also without fear. In bourgeois realism his is a strange borderline case: Flaubert's portrayal of society hints occasionally at the coming dichotomy, but it preserves much of the richness and truth-to-life of earlier realism. After Flaubert, new problems come to the fore. But, before entering into these, it may be useful to instance the tendencies running counter to realism in the literature of the age.

At the time when Heine was composing his later works— about a decade after the above confession—another writer put down his views on the subject—Dostoevsky, in his story *From the Darkness of the City*. This story contains perhaps the first authentic description of the isolation of modern bourgeois man— an interesting ideological link between Dostoevsky and modernism. Yet Dostoevsky still sees such isolation in a social context. He does not idealize it; rather, he paints it in a pessimistic hue and shows it to be a blind alley. The social circumstances and consequences of this isolation are clearly seen by Dostoevsky— where modernism would tend to mystify. His hero's sufferings derive from the inhumanity of early capitalism, and particularly from its destructive influence on personal relationships. Dostoevsky loathes capitalism with all his being; but he rejects a socialist solution no less passionately. His protest against the inhumanity of capitalism is transformed into a sophistical, anti-capitalist romanticism, into a critique of socialism and democracy. Thus, fear of socialism completes the isolation of man in capitalist society (though with Dostoevsky this isolation is to some extent concealed by his pan-Slav clerical mysticism).

Dostoevsky represents, of course, a comparatively early stage in this evolution. Nietzsche, who substitutes a critique of bourgeois philistinism for this critique of bourgeois inhumanity, generalizes the attitude towards life described in Dostoevsky's story, *The Cellar*. This is not the place to show how Nietzsche's identification of capitalism and socialism, his raising of the spectre of 'mass culture', his rejection of democracy and progress, helped to prepare the way for Hitler's demagogy. I attempted this in my book, *The Destruction of Reason*. There, I tried to show how these tendencies had lived on in a modified form after Hitler's defeat. The opposition to socialism gathered momentum and was soon transformed into an ideological crusade which, though nominally concerned with the preservation of democracy, was really nourished by a growing fear of the threat which mass society poses to the ruling elite. If we add to this the dark shadows cast by the nuclear bomb, it will easily be understood how the fear thus engendered could be yoked to acquiescence in, or active support for, Cold War policies.

If I have anticipated a little, it is to point to the final implications of this ideology. I do not suggest that there is a direct connection between modernist literature and political attitudes of this kind. The works of Joyce and Kafka were written long before; and Robert Musil, for example, is known to have been a strong opponent of Nazism. We are not here concerned with directly political attitudes, but rather with the ideology underlying these artists' presentation of reality. The practical political conclusions drawn by the individual writer are of secondary interest. What matters is whether his view of the world, as expressed in his writings, connives at that modern nihilism from which both Fascism and Cold War ideology draw their strength.

There is a close connection between such a view of the world and the rejection of a socialist perspective. We are not concerned with academic discussions about the correctness or otherwise of socialist theory; this need have little bearing on a writer's understanding and portrayal of his age. It is a writer's actual experience of life that interests us. For Heine, on his sickbed, this problem was no less existential than for the hero of Dostoevsky's short story. And it is certainly no less so for the contemporary writer. His, and his heroes', most immediate experience is of their isolation in a world which has become increasingly abstract, uniform, technological. At first these new forces seemed to threaten only his individual culture. Later, they were seen to undermine the foundations of his moral and physical being. Finally, in the nuclear age, the perspective became the destruction of mankind itself.

Every writer has now to face the challenge of this perspective —whether or not he is aware of its social and historical circumstances. Many individual reactions seem at first sight to represent no more than the personal experience of the writers in question. And they are, of course, personal in the sense that all individual experience is unique, that a man cannot jump over his own shadow. But art implies a relation between the artist and the outer world. Indeed, whatever the private opinion of the artist, a relation of some kind is inevitable. And no less inevitable is the imposition of a certain level of generalization on the subject-matter; whether he will or no, every writer describes the condition of mankind. The present social condition of mankind is at the root of even the most abstract, the most solipsistic vision of the future. And since, in the age of imperialism, of world war and world revolution, no search for a valid perspective can overlook socialism, we are entitled to guess at a rejection of socialism behind the fashionable condition of *angst*.

Put in general terms this may sound paradoxical. But examination of individual cases tends to confirm it. We have already encountered Gottfried Benn's notion of '*doppelleben*', of statism (as against dynamics). In his essay, *Can artists change the world?*, Benn examines this problem without mystification or modernist obscurantism—indeed with a surprisingly oldfashioned lucidity.

> I am struck by the thought that it might be more revolutionary and worthier of a vigorous and active man to teach his fellow-men this simple truth: you are what you are and you will never be different; this is, was, and always will be your life. He who has money, lives long; he who has authority; can do no wrong; he who has might, establishes right. Such is history! Ecce historia! Here is the present; take of its body, eat, and die.

The triviality of this, its portentous, affectedly paradoxical tone need not be enlarged on. But it may serve as a key to some of Benn's darker utterances. It may explain the cynicism which led Benn to tolerate the social evils of his time—even collaborating with Hitler—causing him to justify the most dishonourable courses of action as morally permissible, or even desirable. If men and society are basically unchangeable, what other course is there but to collaborate with the powers that be? Seen in this light, Benn's static view of the world is the more easily understandable.

Other modernist pronouncements may be clothed in more mystical language; but they come to the same thing. The German writer Alfred Andersch, for instance, sees—not without justification—the emergence of abstract art as a 'reaction, instinctive or conscious, against the corruption of idea into ideology'. Its contemporary triumph he explains in this way: 'Since the danger of a relapse into totalitarianism is always present, abstract art retains its topicality.' What is meant by the transformation of idea into ideology? Above all, I think, a rejection of socialism. Socialism has forced a bourgeoisie which long since ceased to be revolutionary to reconsider the social roots and consequences of 'ideas'. Traditional bourgeois culture proceeded on the assumption that ideas were not relevant to social or political problems. The dominant view was that they not only could not, but should not, have such relevance. True, men of prophetic insight like Heine and Dostoevsky saw that the advent of socialism would give ideas a new importance and a new relation to reality —or, rather, that socialism would take up the threads of the tradition of the bourgeoisie itself. For nobody doubted, in the 17th and 18th centuries, that the ideas of Hobbes and Milton, of Diderot and Rousseau, strongly influenced, in conjunction with the social movements of the time, men's decisions and actions. It was only later, when the bourgeoisie had won its battle, and the proletariat was still politically and ideologically weak, that the condition which Andersch idealizes came to rule supreme.

Socially speaking, this corruption of idea into ideology has two faces. First, individual ideas are inextricably linked with the social class whose aspirations they express. Second, the struggle between conflicting ideas is ultimately decided by the outcome of the conflict between social classes. This new state of affairs, the renewed relevance of ideas in practical politics, was not properly understood by the bourgeois intelligentsia until the First World War. When, after 1917, the revolutionary outbreaks suddenly revealed that this relation had already existed for some time, the bourgeoisie were forced to face up to the phenomenon. Since bourgeois ideology, however, had at its disposal no ideas of the same calibre as socialism, it generated the 'ideologies'—in the pejorative sense of the term—of Hitlerism and, later, of nuclear catastrophists, whose cynical logic can be found in James Burnham. Then, by way of self-defence, socialism too was declared an 'ideology'.

Inevitably, the leading bourgeois intellectuals were forced to take these changes into account in their writing. And yet, in spite of the evident urgency of the task, there has not yet appeared a system of ideas which could be successfully opposed to socialism. The most typical reactions are either cynicism, as with Gottfried Benn, or a panic-stricken *angst* in the face of Nothingness, leading to the wholesale rejection both of new social forces and of new methods to defend the old society. Andersch is right to imply that abstract art is not wholly without content, that it represents a revolt against what he calls 'ideology'. I have shown what is involved in the process which Andersch, without admittedly fully grasping it, attempts to describe. But it is all too evident that the end-product of this flight from the reality of the present day must be a form of nihilism. Once a commitment to the realities of the age is refused, human content disappears.

In his essay on Beckett, the French critic Maurice Nadeau in effect follows up Andersch's point. Beckett's literary production, he says, took a course which made him 'abandon the conventional fields of literature and penetrate deeper and deeper into that zone of darkness, into that border region where language fails, where life and death meet, where existence and consciousness dissolve and the explorer's path leads to the ante-chamber of silence, of pure reality'. Nadeau, too, speaks of a 'protest'; but this protest is 'voiced by nobody, it has no aim, no reason'. Again: 'enveloped in eternal nothingness, we are no more than bubbles that burst on the surface of a muddy pool, producing that faint sound we call existence.' He sums up: 'with Beckett, triumphant nihilism penetrates into the work of art itself, dissolving the thing it creates into a fog of meaninglessness. In the end, the author has not only made plain his intention not to say anything; he has succeeded in not saying anything. The sound of his voice in our ears is our own voice sought for and found at last.' Here is the logical conclusion of that movement to whose starting-point Andersch drew our attention.

Of course, there are many bourgeois writers who have grasped the implications of this process quite clearly and do not belittle it by indulging in a comfortable nihilism. Louis Bromfield, to take an example at random, attempted in his novel *Mr. Smith* a portrayal of Babbitt twenty years on. The book is of no great artistic merit; but it has some relevance to our investigation. Bromfield noted that in the course of two decades Babbitt's social position had changed considerably: 'His particular features and his particular problems have been undermined by disease and mental confusion without the victim's knowing it. Babbitt was crude in his way, but healthy.' (This is not, perhaps, entirely true. Sinclair Lewis had already pointed out the inherent morbidity of the type.) Now, according to Bromfield, disease is rampant, covering ever greater areas of American life. He remarks, 'In my view, our society is diseased because it is composed of stupid, gutless, extraverted individuals who frequent clubs, gambling houses, brothels, nightclubs, and bars because they are scared ... They are obsessed with movies, with television, with sport; they are in the grip of a deep, instinctive fear. But fear of what?' His novel, which describes the downfall of Mr. Smith, sets out to find the answer.

Bromfield's novel hints unexpectedly at an inner connection between Babbitt and the ethics of modernism. His hero remembers an incident (a drinking and whoring excursion to escape the tedium of family life): 'When I think of this trip I always think of one of those surrealist paintings which show a maze of narrow streets with dazzling neon signs blazing "Pleasure Haunt" or "The Wild Man". From narrow alley-ways and entrances, innumerable phantom arms reach out and pull you from your course. It is how the world appears to a drunken man.' Bromfield explains how Mr. Smith, during a critical phase of his life, comes to prefer Proust to all other writers: Proust is the only writer in whose work 'boredom and fascination are in perfect balance'. Mr. Smith's affection for Proust is not at all literary: 'I discovered in him a life which, though decadent, was as rich and fascinating as my own everyday routine, from the day I first saw myself in the mirror, was mechanical, sterile, dreary.' This suggests, incidentally, that modernist art does not necessarily have a minority appeal. Modernist literature glorifies, with sophisticated artistry, phenomena which must otherwise appear nightmarish to the intellectual who has no perspective of the future. While traditional critical realism transforms the positive and negative elements of bourgeois life into 'typical' situations and reveals them for what they are, modernism exalts bourgeois life's very baseness and emptiness with its aesthetic devices. This tendency began with Naturalism, and has since become widespread, both as regards progressive reduction of content and increasing technical refinement.

In his novel, Bromfield touches on an important problem facing the bourgeois artist. The possibility of realism, as we know, is bound up with that minimal hope of a change for the better offered by bourgeois society. We have seen that in modernist art this perspective disappears altogether. The structure of *L'Education Sentimentale* shows that Flaubert had anticipated this development. The realistic part of the novel ends during the night on the barricades, as Frédéric Moreau watches Dussardier fall, crying 'Vive la republique!', and recognizes in the police agent his former 'radical' comrade Sénécal. The realistic novel is done with; Frédéric Moreau begins his *'Recherche du temps perdu'*.

The end of Bromfield's novel points back once more to Sinclair Lewis; this time not to *Babbitt* but to *Arrowsmith*. The subject of that novel was the position of the scientist under American capitalism. Lewis proposed that those scientists who wished to avoid corruption should escape to the solitude of the forests. Bromfield's hero, too, runs away from a society whose problems he cannot solve: he perishes miserably on a desert island during the Second World War. The difference between the endings of the two novels points to the changes that have come over society in the twenty years Bromfield surveys. Sinclair Lewis uses a mistaken, and certainly untypical, social perspective which does nevertheless give a faithful picture of preceding social developments. With Bromfield the same perspective is the symbol of an ineluctable, total fiasco.

This somewhat negative background had to be sketched in to complete our survey of perspective in bourgeois realism up to the present day. Not a few writers of the transitional period tried to give their encounter with the new situation conceptual form. Ibsen, for example, said: 'My concern is to put questions, not to supply answers.' And Chekhov declared: 'Only the question a writer puts must be reasonable. In many cases, even with Tolstoy, the answers are unreasonable. But that does not invalidate the work in question as long as it is based on a reasonable question.' The instances we have drawn from Sinclair Lewis serve to illustrate these remarks. I have already said why I think the solution in *Arrowsmith* is mistaken; and the note on which *Babbitt* ends —the sons will find the answers to the questions their fathers found too difficult—is altogether too naïve. And yet Ibsen and Chekhov are not wrong. To reject the perspective offered by Sinclair Lewis in his two novels is not to disregard what was nevertheless achieved in them.

The connection should now be apparent between Chekhov's 'reasonable question' and our earlier conclusion that a wholesale rejection of socialism will prevent the writer from giving a realistic account of the modern world. A view of the world based on chaos and *angst* presupposes the elimination of all social categories. Objective reality, we found, in the modernist writing we examined, is subjectivized and robbed of its historicity. Yet, while chaos and *angst* are the inevitable consequences of such subjectivization, their specific content, mood and ideological basis are determined by the social conditions in which the intellectual finds himself. Rejecting with passion or cynicism a socialist perspective, he fails to answer its challenge, refusing both an ideological apology for imperialism and any attempt to find a new perspective for capitalism. Even Koestler, that passionate opponent of Marxism, admitted that after his break with the Party he felt 'God's throne was empty'. The sharp discrepancy between the official ideologies of modern imperialism (Hitler's social demagogy, Burnham's managerial revolution, Democracy versus Communism etc.), and the ideology that underlies so much of contemporary bourgeois literature, is a most significant feature of our time.

That is why both our adaptation of Chekhov's 'reasonable question' and our apparently rather negative conclusion—that non-rejection of socialism is a sufficient basis for realism—are relevant and important. We must not, though, lose sight of the historical nature of our criterion; we are concerned with concrete tendencies, evolving out of actual societies, not with two rigidly opposed metaphysical entities. In my view, the criterion has increasing relevance in our study of the contemporary world; but I would admit that intellectual and social development varies in pace from country to country. There are, even in Europe, countries where feudalism is still powerful; in these the writer in opposition can still conceive of the new society in a bourgeois perspective. We have only to think of Lorca's magnificent *Bernarda Alba's House*, strikingly similar in style and theme to some of Ostrovsky's plays, and yet undeniably an organic product of modern Spanish society. In the nature of the case, such examples are comparatively rare in contemporary European literature. But they are numerous among the backward nations now attaining independence. It is perilous to generalize here; developments in India, for instance, show that socialism may figure among the forces working against medievalism. The unusual character of this social evolution will no doubt give rise to equally unusual literary developments, not to be fitted into any of our existing abstract categories.

But in treating literary developments even in highly-developed capitalist societies we must not forget that we are dealing with developments in history; and historical study demands concrete examples. I referred, earlier, to Sinclair Lewis. His perspective is unquestionably, indeed exclusively, bourgeois. Where their illusions are the main theme ('things like that can't happen to us

. . .'), the book is condemned to mediocrity. But where they are
no more than a rather abstract perspective, Chekhov's notion of
the 'reasonable question' appears to be justified—and justified
very much in the spirit of our argument. For Sinclair Lewis'
views do not amount to a rejection of socialism; at most, he drops
the occasional ironic remark about such manifestations of
socialism as he knew.

With Joseph Conrad, matters are rather more complex. Conrad was firmly opposed to socialism; and this opposition is
evident in some of his writings, often causing a certain distortion
(*The Nigger of the Narcissus, Under Western Eyes*). Yet in his
best writings a strange phenomenon is observable: his faith in
capitalism is such that the narrative does not even touch on its
social implications. Conrad's heroes are confronted with exclusively personal, moral conflicts, in which their individual
strength or weakness is revealed. Put in more general terms these
conflicts might have attained a wider significance; but such
generalization is excluded by the method of narration. This gives
Conrad's work its finished, self-sufficient quality, but it also prevents him from portraying the totality of life; he is really a short-
story writer rather than a novelist. *Typhoon* or *The Shadow
Line* are famous examples; but even *Lord Jim* is, despite its length,
essentially a long short-story. Thus Conrad's 'reasonable question', though excluding the most important social problems of
his time, makes possible that 'triumph of realism' we find in him.
It eliminated just those ideological elements which might have
inhibited a truthful description of the life of his age.

Our interest centres, then, on the relation between ideology
(in the sense of *Weltanschauung*) and artistic creation. Ideology
has here a double significance. There are, first, a writer's conscious views about life and the problems of his time. Second,
there is the understanding and portrayal of these things in his
work. It was Engels who pointed out that the two might actually
be diametrically opposed (I may refer the reader to my analysis of
Tolstoy and Balzac in *Studies in European Realism*). This opposition takes different forms at different periods; and, even at one

71

and the same period, the opposition varies according to the personality and views of the writer in question. I want at this point,
though, to reject the opposition of perception and emotion which
has become so fashionable. This, though it may indeed occur
in individual writers, cannot but have a bad effect on their work.
Experience shows that, in any artistically fruitful opposition,
both poles are invested with perception-based-on-emotion and
emotion-become-perception—Heine's work is a good example of
this.

It would be interesting to examine Hemingway, Steinbeck,
or Thomas Wolfe in this light; bearing in mind that the analysis
must always be geared to the specific character of a writer's production. Our examination of Conrad is only one example; it
should not be taken as a model. But I think the relevance of our
criterion could be established in all these cases. Thomas Mann's
artistic development, illustrates too, the historical nature of our
criterion. *Buddenbrooks* still belongs, of course, to Mann's early
period. But directly before and during the First World War Mann
began to introduce socialism into the world portrayed in his
writings. And, from the *Magic Mountain* onwards, socialism
never ceases to be a central intellectual and compositional element.

The negatively formulated 'reasonable question' of contemporary realism—no *a priori* rejection of socialism—has as its complement another negative imperative: the will to overcome
angst and chaos. I have tried to show that these form the essential
content of modernism. This vision of the world as chaos results
from the lack of a humanist social perspective. The self-deception
from which modernism suffers in this respect is based on
a peculiar, and contradictory, piece of dogmatism. To modernists, though they are almost without exception supporters of
extreme subjectivism, the static nature of reality, and the sense-
lessness of its surface phenomena, are absolute truths requiring
no proof. Naturally, phenomena in the outer world, governed by
their own immanent laws, exist outside human consciousness.
But the human subject plays a part in the understanding of

particular phenomena and in the perception of their interrelatedness. As Hegel said, 'He who looks at the world rationally, finds in it a rational pattern; the two processes are one.'

In the same way, the reason for the part played in modernist art by *angst* is not to be found in the dogma that reality is chaos. Rather, inability to grasp the new pattern of social development leads to an *angst*-ridden view of reality. *Angst*, of course, derives from an experience in the outer world; but this experience is of its nature subjective and results from a certain way of looking at reality. Kierkegaard, the prophet of this experience, comments: '... Nothingness, the object of *angst*, gradually becomes an entity.... The Nothingness that results from *angst* is a complex of subjective fears, reflecting one another and gradually closing in on the individual....' We see that, contrary to the dogma, *angst* precedes chaos in modernist ideology. Chaos is the consequence of *angst*; and *angst* in turn is the product of social experience—the effect, specifically, of the social structure of imperialism on the bourgeois intelligentsia. Rejection of socialism as a possible perspective involves closing one's eyes to the future; the individual then accepts *angst* and chaos as a permanent condition. It is not, I think, necessary to analyse the ideology further. Earlier in this study I contrasted those two fundamentally opposed ontologies, Aristotelianism and Existentialism. Let us now look at the matter in a rather broader context.

Angst, as a dominant existential condition, leads to an impoverishment, reduction and distortion of the image of man and of described reality. It excludes everything lying beyond its own radius, and particularly—a natural consequence of its origin—everything that invests man and his environment with social significance. This process continues through the imperialist period. It is latent in Naturalism, reaching a culmination in the later works of Strindberg. Earlier, in the plays of the young Maeterlinck, it had already found authentic form. *Angst*, in the shape of a disturbing premonition or vague *sehnsucht*, had been the effective content of much Naturalistic literature; with Maeterlinck it became the exclusive content, displacing all other aspirations. Beckett's *Waiting for Godot*, whatever variations it may offer in style and mood, is essentially very close to early Maeterlinck.

A new feature in the later stages of this process is the increasing exclusiveness, the radical, almost brutal elimination of social significance. Take, for instance, D. H. Lawrence's reduction of erotic relations to phallic sexuality, or the even more extreme version of this reduction in Henry Miller. The German critic Helmut Uhlig gives this description of Miller's world: 'Contempt for work, drink as a drug, sexual intercourse as the raison d'etre of existence, promiscuity as a way of life, reliance on all manner of violent stimuli.' And he goes on to quote Miller on his own experience of life: 'The world came to resemble a pornographic film, with impotence as its tragic theme.' Uhlig points out that similarities can be found in the works, say, of Broch, Kafka, and Musil. Impotence is thought of not so much as a physical failure, but rather as 'a man's emotional failure to establish contact with a woman; a betrayal of woman, who— with Miller—is degraded into a mere object, and valued for her sexual capacity alone'. These comments, coming as they do from a non-socialist, confirm our point. The tendency I am describing is, of course, a good deal more complex in writers of greater talent and intelligence than Henry Miller. And the reduction of which I have spoken does not necessarily relate, as Beckett's example shows, only to sexuality.

Yet this reduction is here the ultimate determinant of literary style. Earlier in this study I discussed the question of narrative detail and its place in the totality of the work of art and concluded that the rejection of a selective principle must lead the modernist writer to naturalism, even where the experimental form would lead one to expect the opposite. We can now take these findings a stage further: the selective principle which apparently underlies modernist writing is no more than a crude selection of content, on the one hand, and of technique, on the other. It is not a selection applied to the totality of the reality to be described. In genuine selection, insignificant data are eliminated and significant data stressed. In modernism, purely formal principles of selection lead to a fragmentation of human nature (Henry Miller, for instance, ignores everything in human nature that cannot be related to sexuality). A pseudo-selection of this kind degrades the human image, eliminating much that is of the essence of man.

The problem of narrative detail, of naturalism, has thus to be seen in a wider context. Since human nature is not finally separable from social reality, each narrative detail will be significant to the extent that it expresses the dialectic between man-as-individual and man-as-social-being. It is these tensions and contradictions both within the individual, and underlying the individual's relation with his fellow human beings—all of which tensions increase in intensity with the evolution of capitalism—that must form the subject-matter of contemporary realism. The realistic writer must seek the nodal points of these conflicts, determine where they are at their most intense and most typical, and give suitable expression to them. Good realistic detail often in itself implies a judgment on these conflicts. The question of what we mean by the *norm*, and by *distortion*, is also involved.

These categories—norm and distortion—can be used to determine an individual's relation to society; but they can only do this if the literary technique allows of equal treatment being given to both aspects of human nature. A realistic work of art, however rich in descriptive detail, is always opposed to naturalism. But an artistic method which reduces the dialectical—social-and-individual—totality of human existence must relapse, as we have seen, into naturalistic arbitrariness. It will then be incapable of depicting distortion in human nature or in the individual's relation to his environment—incapable, that is, of seeing distortion as distortion.

Once again we observe the profoundly anti-artistic character of modernism. The historical legitimation of modernism derives from the fact that the distortion of human nature, the anti-artistic character of human relationships, is an inevitable product of capitalist society. Yet since modernism portrays this distortion without critical detachment, indeed devises stylistic techniques which emphasize the necessity of distortion in any kind of society, it may be said to distort distortion further. By attributing distortion to reality itself, modernism dismisses the counter-forces at work in reality as ontologically irrelevant. It is easy to understand that the experience of the contemporary capitalist world does produce, especially among intellectuals, *angst*, nausea, a sense of isolation, and despair. Indeed, a view of the world which *excluded* these emotions would prevent the present-day artist from depicting his world truthfully. The question is not: is x present in reality? But rather: does x represent the whole of reality? Again, the question is not; should x be excluded from literature? But rather: should we be content to leave it at x ?

We are brought back once again to questions of ideology. If a writer takes *angst* to be the basic experience of modern man, his attitude towards the life of his time betrays an uncritical naïvety. 'Naïvety' I want here to be understood in a philosophical sense. I went into this concept in my published correspondence with Anna Seghers about realism over two decades ago. I meant by it an attitude which excluded critical detachment, which registered the phenomena of life naïvely, which stuck to first impressions. This attitude, I showed then, may be combined with rigorous scientific investigation—though it will be a scientific activity uncritical of its own assumptions. We cannot go further into the question here—examining to what extent, for instance, this 'naïvety' is a spontaneous reaction of the artist living under capitalism, and to what extent it is deliberately furthered to prevent the artist from criticizing capitalism's presuppositions. I want merely to point out the distinction between a critical and a naïve approach in the present context, in order to clarify its philosophical basis. I would like also to recall our earlier discussion of the connection between realism—i.e. a writer's critical understanding of the world he lives in—and the struggle for peace, which is similarly based on an ideological rejection of assumptions about the inevitability of war which are based on uncritical analysis of reality. The distinction between this approach and that of modernism, which by its nature must be uncritical and naïve in its attitude to reality, should be sufficiently evident.

Franz Kafka is the classic example of the modern writer at the mercy of a blind and panic-stricken *angst*. His unique position he owes to the fact that he found a direct, uncomplex way of communicating this basic experience; he did so without having recourse to formalistic experimentation. Content is here the immediate determinant of aesthetic form—that is why Kafka belongs with the great realistic writers. Indeed, he is one of the greatest of all, if we consider how few writers have ever equalled his skill in the imaginative evocation of the concrete novelty of the world. Never was the quality of Kafka's achievement more striking or more needed than at the present day, when so many writers fall for slick experimentation. The impact of Kafka's work derives not only from his passionate sincerity—rare enough in our age—but also from the corresponding simplicity of the world he constructs. That is Kafka's most original achievement. Kierkegaard said, 'The greater a man's originality, the more he is at the mercy of *angst*.' Kafka, original in the Kierkegaardian sense, describes this *angst* and the fragmented world which—it is incorrectly assumed—is both its complement and its cause. His originality lies not in discovering any new means of expression but in the utterly convincing, and yet continually startling, presentation of his invented world, and of his characters' reaction to it. 'What shocks is not the monstrosity of it,' writes Theodor W. Adorno, 'but its matter-of-factness.'

The diabolical character of the world of modern capitalism, and man's impotence in the face of it, is the real subject-matter of Kafka's writings. His simplicity and sincerity are, of course, the product of complex and contradictory forces. Let us consider only one aspect. Kafka wrote at a time when capitalist society, the object of his *angst*, was still far from the high mark of its historical development. What he described and 'demonized' was not the truly demonic world of Fascism, but the world of the

Hapsburg Monarchy. *Angst*, haunting and indefinable, is perfectly reflected in this vague, ahistorical, timeless world, steeped in the atmosphere of Prague. Kafka profited from his historical position in two ways. On the one hand, his narrative detail gains from being rooted in the Austrian society of that period. On the other hand, the essential unreality of human existence, which it is his aim to convey, can be related to a corresponding sense of unreality and foreboding in the society he knew. The identification with the *condition humaine* is far more convincing than in later visions of a diabolical, *angst*-inspiring world, where so much has to be eliminated or obscured by formal experimentation to achieve the desired ahistorical, timeless image of the human condition. But this, though the reason for the astonishing impact and lasting power of Kafka's work, cannot disguise its basically allegorical character. The wonderfully suggestive descriptive detail points to a transcendent reality, to the anticipated reality—stylized into timelessness—of fully developed imperialism. Kafka's details are not, as in realism, the nodal points of individual or social life; they are cryptic symbols of an unfathomable transcendence. The stronger their evocative power, the deeper is the abyss, the more evident the allegorical gap between meaning and existence.

The counterpart to this fascinating, though ill-starred, development in modern bourgeois literature is the work of Thomas Mann. I have examined Thomas Mann's work extensively elsewhere, and shall be brief. It is only important for our purposes to work out the contrast with Kafka. Let us begin with the artistic presentation. The world of Thomas Mann is free from transcendental reference: place, time and detail are rooted firmly in a particular social and historical situation. Mann envisages the perspective of socialism without abandoning the position of a bourgeois, and without attempting to portray the newly emergent socialist societies or even the forces working towards their establishment (in the context of realism, Thomas Mann's mature attitude of acceptance and resignation, and Roger Martin du Gard's heroic failure, form an interesting opposition).

This apparently limited perspective is nevertheless of central importance in Thomas Mann's work: it is the main reason for the harmony of its proportions. Each section of a portrayed totality is placed in a concrete social context; the significance of each detail, its meaning for the evolution of society, is clearly defined. It is our world that Thomas Mann describes, the world in whose shaping we play a part, and which in turn shapes us. The deeper Thomas Mann probes into the complexity of present-day reality, the more clearly we come to understand our position in the complex evolution of mankind. Thus Thomas Mann, despite his loving attention to detail, never lapses into naturalism. For all his fascination with the dark regions of modern existence, Thomas Mann always shows up distortion for what it is, tracing its roots and its concrete origins in society.

In his study of Dostoevsky, André Gide wrote, 'Beautiful feelings make bad art', and, 'without the devil's help there would be no art'. Some of Thomas Mann's writings are based on not dissimilar views; there are parallels in his early story *Tonio Kröger*. Yet, in the same story, Mann also gives us the opposing view. The problem treated is familiar in the modern world. Thomas Mann is concerned to investigate the demonic, the underworld of the human mind, within the context of present-day society. Early in his career he realized that the artist himself is one of the main mediators of this experience. It is therefore natural that he should have followed up this early insight with increasingly rigorous studies of the problem in its social context. The examination begun with *Tonio Kröger*, ended with *Dr Faustus*. With Adrian Leverkühn, Mann's Faustus, the enquiry is concentrated on the present time, though it is a present seen in the perspective of history. The devil has to confess that, with Goethe, his assistance was strictly unnecessary, but that the social conditions of Leverkühn's time compelled the composer to seek guidance from the underworld. Yet Leverkühn's final monologue reveals the perspective of a new society, of socialism, under which the artist will be freed from his former enslavement. Indeed, the mere struggle for the social reformation of mankind may of itself suffice to break the power of the underworld.

Gide's attitude to the problem, as we saw from the above remarks, was 'naïve', uncritical. He surrendered to the supremacy of the underworld, greeted it even with a certain intellectual relish, and with the customary contempt for the trivial philistinism of bourgeois existence. Gide's notion of the *action gratuite* reflects the same view, as does his doctrine of 'sincerity'. What in Mann is simply one legitimate theme among others—legitimate even where it is the main theme of a novel or story—becomes with Gide a doctrine governing all life and all art—and thus distorting both. This is the crossroads where critical realism not only parts ways with modernism, but is even forced into opposition to it.

Between these methods, between Franz Kafka and Thomas Mann, the contemporary bourgeois writer will have to choose. There is no necessity for a writer to break with his bourgeois pattern of life in making this choice between social sanity and morbidity, in choosing the great and progressive literary traditions of realism in preference to formalistic experimentation. (Of course, there are many writers who will choose socialism as a way of solving their personal dilemma. I only want to emphasize that this is not the only possible choice for the contemporary writer.) What counts is the personal decision. Chekhov's 'reasonable question' implies, above all, a choice of direction. And today that is determined by the question: acceptance or rejection of *angst*? Ought *angst* to be taken as an absolute, or ought it to be overcome? Should it be considered one reaction among others, or should it become the determinant of the *condition humaine*? These are not primarily, of course, literary questions; they relate to a man's behaviour and experience of life. The crucial question is whether a man escapes from the life of his time into a realm of abstraction—it is then that *angst* is engendered in human consciousness—or confronts modern life determined to fight its evils and support what is good in it. The first decision leads then to another: is man the helpless victim of transcendental and inexplicable forces, or is he a member of a human community in which he can play a part, however small, towards its modification or reform?

These problems could well be expanded and generalized; but it is not necessary to do so here. The implications of our basic question—acceptance of *angst* or rejection—are clear enough. We see here, ideologically and artistically, the root of our modern dilemma. However passionately, however sophistically, the historical origins of *angst* may be obscured, no work of art based on it can avoid—objectively speaking—guilt by association with Hitlerism and the preparations for atomic war. It is, indeed, of the nature of literature's social significance that it reflects the movements of its age even when it is—subjectively—aiming to express something very different (this opposition between subjective intention and objective compulsion is at the root of the modernist dilemma: modernism is in revolt against the anti-aestheticism of capitalism, and yet in the process revolts against art itself).

Earlier, I quoted Adorno's remark that modern music had lost the original authenticity of *angst*. This, and similar instances, being interpreted, could well be taken as an admission of defeat in the field of nuclear war preparations, an admission of loss of ground in the Cold War, as new perspectives for peace begin to open up. Modernism, based on nihilism, is losing that suggestive power which contrived to invest Nothingness with a false objectivity. The experience of Nothingness, though distorting reality when made use of in literature, did possess a certain subjective authenticity. This authenticity, however, has diminished with time. Thus, as the crisis of modernism deepens, critical realism grows in importance.

Let me repeat: these changes are primarily changes in human behaviour, in ideological attitude; only by this route can they affect literature. Moreover, I would like the reader to recall what I said earlier about the peculiar ideological pattern underlying the Peace Movement: how it allows great ideological divergencies, even contradictions, holding together differing approaches by a certain community of opinion on human, social, and international problems. Chekhov's 'reasonable question', which we found to be the basis of all realistic literature, is the theoretical link between a community of opinion of this kind and the creative process itself.

It is evident that changes of this sort must be complex and contradictory. They may involve the gradual transformation of a writer's understanding of the social and historical reality of his time (Thomas Mann, for instance, during and after the First World War). A writer's earlier views will not necessarily be abandoned in their entirety, even if these views are really inseparable from the abandoned intellectual position (e.g. Thomas Mann's continued attachment to Schopenhauer and Nietzsche). One result, in the field of theory, is likely to be the partial break-up of the earlier ideology—as with Sartre, whose political views are often inconsistent with his unrevised existentialist premisses. A writer faced with this dilemma may yet succeed in formulating his 'reasonable question' on the basis of his new position. The problems he leaves unsolved may appear in his work as truthful reflections of contradictions actually present in society. Sartre's work provides evidence of this.

Apparent inconsistencies in a writer's view of the world, reflected in his work, should never be treated dogmatically. The main thing—and it is no small thing—is whether the writer's view is able to include—or, better, demands—a dynamic, complex, analytical rendering of social relationships, or whether it leads to loss of perspective and historicity. We are confronted once again with an alternative—acceptance of *angst* or rejection—and with all the consequences flowing from that alternative. This dilemma is the key to the assessment of modern literature.

It is applicable, not least, in matters of style. Earlier, in talking of the historical and aesthetic significance of certain stylistic phenomena, I rejected any rigid distinction, on formal principles alone, between bourgeois realism and decadent anti-realism. In a period of transition, when the rejection of old beliefs and the formulation of new beliefs is a continuous process, this negative principle of judgment becomes more, rather than less, important. Crucial, for the critic, is the determination of the direction in which a writer is moving, not the detection of stylistic idiosyncrasies. This is not to say that style is unimportant. On the contrary, I maintain that the more closely we combine an examination of the ideology informing a writer's work with an examination of the specific form given to a specific content, the better our analysis will be. That is to say, the critic must establish by examination of the work whether a writer's view of the world is based on the acceptance or rejection of *angst*, whether it involves a flight from reality or a willingness to face up to it.

The more *angst* predominates, the greater will be the levelling effect. We have seen this in the case of abstract and concrete potentiality. But the loss of any concern for ethical complexity, for the problems of society, is part of the same process. The question of the 'authenticity' of human behaviour is no longer important. Particularly in modernist writing, the differing reactions of human beings come to seem insignificant in the face of 'metaphysical' *angst* (and of the increasing pressures of conformity). The fact that in the midst of this 'permanent revolution', this endless 'revaluation of all values', there were writers of major talent who clung to the standards of nineteenth-century realism is, therefore, of ethical as much as of artistic significance. These writers' attitudes sprang from the ethical conviction that though changes in society modify human nature, they do not abolish it. Once again, Roger Martin du Gard is the classic example. The conviction is evident, not only in his thinking about literature, but also in the values inherent in his work. We have only to contrast the tragic authenticity of his Jacques Thibault with the inauthenticity of his Fontanin, who embodies the Gidean ethic.

But Martin du Gard is by no means the only example. The best work of Eugene O'Neill, an experimentalist from his expressionist period onward, was done under the influence of nineteenth-century, Ibsenite drama. I am not implying that O'Neill, either philosophically or artistically, was an imitator of Ibsen. On the contrary, he does away with Ibsen's moralizing and his weakness for romantic symbolism. The tragicomedy of Ibsen's stern imperatives, too, is foreign to O'Neill's drama. O'Neill's tragicomedy has been through the school of Chekhov. The ethical-dramatic dialectic is no longer that between absolute imperatives and the impossibility of their realization. We are now concerned with the scope and possibilities of human action as such; O'Neill's subject is man himself, his subjectively tragic and yet objectively comic situation. Again, to say that O'Neill drew inspiration from Chekhov is not to accuse him of imitation. The America he portrays is, sociologically, that described by his contemporaries—though he often, to win dramatic distance, sets the scene in the America of the past. But he is interested not so much in the way human beings can be manipulated in the name of 'Freedom', as in whether, and how, the human substance can survive such a process. O'Neill wishes to know whether a man is in the last analysis responsible for his own actions or is the plaything of psychological and social forces over which he has no control. His American Electra acknowledges responsibility for her actions with tragic pride; the integrity of human personality is preserved, though at great cost. But such a situation is unusual in O'Neill. More often, the authentic and the inauthentic are inextricably interwoven in his characters— the accent falling more and more frequently on the latter. That is O'Neill's originality. Seeing the situation as he does, he is yet able to affirm, with his own brand of tragicomic defiance, a basic integrity in human personality. For all the apparent gloom, this is the message of later dramas like A Moon for the Misbegotten or A Touch of the Poet. In other words, O'Neill's return to Ibsen and Chekhov is at the same time a protest against the dominance of modernism and a confession of faith in the future of humanity.

Stylistically, Elsa Moranti, the Italian novelist, might seem a far cry from O'Neill. Her technique is very much of the present day; little would seem to associate her with the literature of the nineteenth century. All the more striking, then, the philosophical and ethical affinities apparent in her treatment of motive and perspective. Life and its turmoils, in her work, are the threshing-floor where the authentic is winnowed from the inauthentic. Her best-known novel is entitled, significantly, *Lies and Magic*. The plot is intelligent, finely symbolic, excellently suited to the problems she examines. She decribes in the opening chapters the inner revolt of a human being, caught in a net of magic and unreality, against these entangling forces. The '*recherche du temps perdu*' is here no more than a prelude, an introductory evocation of the past—but of the past as it really was, and as none of the characters in the story could have known it from personal experience. Thus, the true subject-matter of the story, the world of *temps retrouvé* is not reduced to a mere *état d'âme*. The motives are derived from actual life; they are the passions, though informed by 'false consciousness', that are at the root of men's actions. The reader—as in the traditional epic —is granted an omniscience allowing him to see the totality of the world portrayed. The winnowing of the authentic from the inauthentic is not effected by the personal intervention of the author. It is the concrete contradictions embodied in her characters, their complex interrelations, that accomplish the process. The novel becomes, in fact, a grandiose parable of modern man's ethical condition. This parabolic quality might seem to yield a point of contact with modernism. But the resemblance does not go very deep; it is confined to the depiction of general background rather than to the portrayal of individuals. The social pressures on the individual are never abstractly conceived—the chief temptation of the parabolic form. The characters' rootedness in their milieu is rendered with remarkable skill. Purely individual and purely class characteristics, carefully distinguished, are yet fused in a unity rarely found outside classical realism. The parabolic quality of the whole is '*aufgehoben*', in the Hegelian sense, in three ways: it is 'cancelled out', yet also preserved; and at the same time it is raised to a higher level—a level where life, and philosophical reflection upon it, form a dialectical unity.

Thomas Wolfe's novel *You Can't Go Home Again* deserves a brief mention here, since it illustrates the turning point in his life so well. Wolfe has described how he began his career as a disciple of Joyce; but his substitution of the *monologue intérieur* for the formal rigours of plot has, in actual fact, a quite different character. It is never a mere stream of consciousness behind which objective reality disappears. The real subject-matter, even of the young Thomas Wolfe, is the reality of modern America; and the stream of consciousness is no more than a part of this objectively-rendered whole. Wolfe's early style, still Joycean but already pointing beyond Joyce, must be seen in relation to his general philosophical stance. Wolfe was passionately involved in the life of his time; but his hates and enthusiasms were on a level of pure emotion. Joyce's technique enabled him to react to and record, emotionally and subjectively, the life around him. But he went beyond Joyce in that he was not the uninvolved spectator of his age. Rather, he was impelled by—admittedly largely unconscious—ethical and social motives either furiously to reject or furiously to affirm what he saw. In his last novel, this unawareness of his own motives has gone. The experience of the Depression, and later of Nazi Germany, revealed to him the make-up of the society of which he was a member. This new understanding enabled him to order and clarify his emotions. The result is the magnificent portrait—particularly in the first half of the book—of America on the eve of the 1929 disaster. But the second half of the book shows that the awareness was not yet complete. By giving his fictive hero certain features obviously taken from Sinclair Lewis, Wolfe attempts to set up a new ideal of what the writer should be. His hero achieves what the young Wolfe had longed for—fame. But fame, when found, is not enough to slake his ambition. Wolfe offers, then, a somewhat abstract solution—he argues that 'one can and should better the human lot', that there is a greater wisdom than the wisdom of Ecclesiastes. This enables him to give, for instance, splendidly realized descriptions of conditions in the

Third Reich. But the second half of the novel is artistically chaotic and leans far too heavily, towards the end, on mere discussion. It must be said, nevertheless, that Thomas Wolfe's death robbed us of a realistic writer of the first promise.

In Brecht's development, too, traditional realism played an important role. I have no space here to examine Brecht's work at length. We must begin with Brecht's middle period, the period of his turning towards communism, of *The Measures Taken* and of his adaptation of Gorky's *Mother*. Brecht's political didacticism, his attempt to impose intellectual schemata on the spectator, turned his characters into mere spokesmen. He based his new aesthetic on a contempt for cheap theatrical emotionalism. The full blast of his hatred was directed towards the 'culinary' aspects of the contemporary bourgeois theatre. And he seized on the theory of *Einfühlung* as the source of much of the bad art of the time. Now there is no doubt that Brecht, despite his exaggerations, was right to reject this particular theory. But he made the then not uncommon mistake—implicit in Wilhelm Worringer's original formulation of the theory—of assuming that *Einfühlung* was fundamental to traditional aesthetics. The boss's secretary may 'identify', through *Einfühlung*, with her opposite number on the screen; and the young man about town may identify with, say, Schnitzler's *Anatol*. But no one surely has ever, in this sense, 'identified' with Antigone or King Lear. The truth is, Brecht's dramatic theories were the product of an—at the time, quite justified—local polemic. Brecht's actual dramatic practice changed radically after the rise to power of Hitler, during his long years of exile. But he never subjected his theories to revision. I have no space to investigate the problem in detail. But two poems, written during that exile, may serve to indicate the changes I have in mind:

> A wooden Japanese mask hangs on my wall
> The mask of an angry demon, covered with gold.
> With fellow-feeling I see
> The swollen veins in the forehead, showing
> What a strenuous business it is to be angry.

87

Or these lines from the marvellous poem *To Posterity:*

> Yet we know too well,
> Hatred of evil
> Can distort the features,
> Rage at injustice
> Make the voice hoarse. Alas, we
> Who wished to make room for friendliness
> Could not ourselves be friendly.

We see here how ethical preoccupations, a concern for the inner life and motivation of his characters, began to loom larger in Brecht's mind. Not that his central political and social preoccupations were displaced. On the contrary, the effect of this change was to give them greater depth, range and intensity. And even the greatest admirers of Brecht's dramaturgy must admit that many plays of this period—*The Rifles of Señora Carrar* or *The Life of Galileo*—evidence a partial return to despised Aristotelean aesthetics. Be that as it may, let us briefly turn our attention to those plays—*Mother Courage, The Caucasian Chalk Circle, The Good Woman of Setzuan*—which do not thus return to traditional norms. These plays are indeed *Lehrstücke*, products of epic theatre; the anti-Aristotelean intention, the calculated use of alienation-effects, is undeniable. But if we compare these plays with, say, *The Measures Taken* we see that the over-simplified schema of that play has given way to a complex dialectic of good and evil. Problems of society have become problems of humanity, subsuming the inner conflicts and contradictions of the warring parties. Where Brecht's characters had once been spokesmen for political points of view, they are now multi-dimensional. They are living human beings, wrestling with conscience and with the world around them. Allegory has acquired flesh and blood; it has been transformed into a true dramatic typology. Alienation-effect ceases to be the instrument of an artificial, abstract didacticism; it makes possible literary achievement of the highest order. All great drama, after all, must find means to transcend the limited awareness of the characters presented on the stage. It must express the general philosophical theme, represented in concrete terms by the action, in adequate poetic form (this is the function of the chorus in Aeschylus and Sophocles, and of the monologue in *Hamlet*, *Othello*, and *Lear*). It is this aspect that predominates in the later Brecht, a direct consequence of his new concern for ethical complexity, of his search for a multi-dimensional typology. That Brecht clung to his earlier theories should not conceal from us this fundamental change. Even the scenic structure of Brecht's plays begins to approximate to the Shakespearean model. The break with the '*milieu*-theatre', with the 'atmospheric' ambience of the older stage, is really a break with naturalism. It is a return to a dramaturgy aiming both at a typology that displays the full range of human complexity and at the creation of living human beings grappling with the forces of their environment. The mature Brecht, by overcoming his earlier, one-sided theories, had evolved into the greatest realistic playwright of his age. And the most influential, too, for good and for bad. Indeed, Brecht's influence shows once again how misleading it is to argue from the theory to the work and not from the work, its structure and intellectual content, to the theory. For Brecht's theories lead both to the pretentious, empty experimentalism of Ionesco and to topical, realistic drama like Dürrenmatt's *The Visit*. The confusion to which this gave rise—the result of a formalistic over-emphasis on one element abstracted from literature—is still remarkably widespread and influential (that Brecht was a socialist writer, both in personal ideology and literary practice, in no way contradicts what I have said here. His influence has been, and is, chiefly effective in the struggle between critical realism and modernist anti-realism).

The critic today must put aside his personal preferences and use all his tact, energy and discretion in evaluating those works of literature which fight against old-established prejudices and strive to open up new areas of experience. To take one example: it is true to say that naturalism represents—compared with true realism—a decline and an impoverishment. In existing conditions, however, a naturalistic novel like Norman Mailer's *The*

Naked and the Dead marks a step forward from the trackless desert of abstractions towards a portrayal of the actual suffering of actual people during the Second World War. Arbitrary though much of the detail is, and retrograde though the author's subsequent artistic development has been, the merits of that achievement, tentative as it was, should not be overlooked. The same may be true even where at first glance there is little evidence of realism. A case in point is *Kimmerische Fahrt*, a novel by the German writer, Werner Warsinsky. Stylistically, this is a competent exercise in the Kafka manner, using techniques evolved by Joyce and Beckett. Formally, the subject would appear to be the *condition humaine* of modernist ideology: there are the same forces working towards man's degradation and ultimate destruction. But the real focus of the book is the hero's experience of the collapse of Nazism; his fate is representative of the fate of a whole generation. The mist and darkness occluding the *angst*-ridden mind of the hero, who is running away from himself and from all contact with the outside world, are the true subject-matter of the book, not a mere stylistic device (though the opposite would seem to be true, if the book is approached from a formal angle). Again, through this mist we catch sight, from time to time, of living human beings, realistically portrayed. As an account of an historical catastrophe the book is excellent. Not dissimilar is the use of dream sequences in Wolfgang Koeppen's *Treibhaus*. Here, the dreamlike atmosphere helps to establish a definite historical atmosphere, while implying a judgment on the dreamlike world of Bonn politics. In his *Tod in Rom* Koeppen goes further in the realism of his treatment of human situation and character. Many other examples, of course, could be found; but the scope of this study does not permit us to take further examples. I want only to point out that these works are the products of a period of transition, and should be investigated as such.

It is a difficult and complex task, yet it is perfectly possible, for a writer to change his attitude to himself, to his fellow human beings, and the world at large. The forces employed against him, admittedly, are enormously powerful. Nihilism and cynicism, despair and *angst*, suspicion and self-disgust are the spontaneous product of the capitalist society in which intellectuals have to live. Many factors, in education and elsewhere, are arrayed against him. Take, for instance, the view that pessimism is aristocratic, a worthier philosophy for an intellectual élite than faith in human progress. Or the belief that the individual—precisely as a member of an élite—must be a helpless victim of historical forces. Or the idea that the rise of mass society is an unmitigated evil. The majority of the press, highbrow and lowbrow, tends to minister to prejudices of this kind (it is their role in the campaign for the continuation of the Cold War). It is as if it were unworthy of the intellectual to hold other than dogmatic modernist views on life, art, and philosophy. To support realism in art, to examine the possibilities of peaceful coexistence among nations, to strive for an impartial evaluation of communism (which does not involve allegiance to it), all this may make a writer an outcast in the eyes of his colleagues and in the eyes of those on whom he depends for a livelihood. Since a writer of Sartre's standing has had to endure attacks of this kind, how much more dangerous is the situation likely to be for younger, less prominent writers.

These, and much more, are hard facts. But we must not forget that strong counter-forces are at work, particularly today; and that they are growing in strength. The writer who considers his own basic interests, those of his nation and of mankind as a whole, and who decides to work against the forces prevailing in the capitalist world, is now no longer alone. The further his explorations take him, the firmer his choice will be, and the less isolated will he feel, for he will be identifying himself with those forces in the world of his time which will one day prevail.

The period during which Fascism rose to power, like the period of Fascist ascendancy and the subsequent Cold War period, were hardly favourable to the growth of critical realism. Nevertheless, excellent work was done; neither physical terror nor intellectual pressure succeeded in preventing it. There were always critical realist writers who opposed war—in both its cold and hot manifestations—and the destruction of art and culture. Not a few works of high artistic merit emerged from the struggle. Today, the imminent defeat of Cold War policies, the new perspective of peaceful coexistence among the nations, should allow wider scope for a critical and realistic bourgeois literature. The real dilemma of our age is not the opposition between capitalism and socialism, but the opposition between peace and war. The first duty of the bourgeois intellectual has become the rejection of an all-pervading fatalistic *angst*, implying a rescue operation for humanity rather than any breakthrough to Socialism. Because it is these perspectives that confront him, the bourgeois writer today is in a better position to solve his own dilemma than he was in the past. It is the dilemma of the choice between an aesthetically appealing, but decadent modernism, and a fruitful critical realism. It is the choice between Franz Kafka and Thomas Mann.

Critical Realism and Socialist Realism

OUR ANALYSIS of critical realism would be incomplete if it were limited to the contrast between critical realism and bourgeois modernism, and not extended to the relation between critical and socialist realism. It is impossible, of course, to go into all the problems of socialist realism in this study. I shall confine myself, therefore, to the relation between the two types of realism and touch only on those aspects of socialist realism which bear on the prospects for critical realism in our time.

Let us first consider the question of *perspective* in critical and socialist realism, as we did when dealing with bourgeois realism and modernism. The perspective of socialist realism is, of course, the struggle for socialism. This perspective will vary in form and content according to the level of social development and the subject-matter. The decisive point—particularly in contrast to critical realism—is not simply the acceptance of socialism. This is possible within the framework of critical realism. An outright affirmation of socialism is not, of course, characteristic of the main body of critical realist writing (I have shown that a negative attitude, readiness to respect the perspective of socialism and not condemn it out of hand, is sufficient). And it is true that such an affirmation will remain somewhat abstract, for even where a critical realist attempts to describe socialism, his is bound to be a description *from the outside.*

That, then, is the crucial distinction. Socialist realism differs from critical realism, not only in being based on a concrete socialist perspective, but also in using this perspective to describe the forces working towards socialism *from the inside.* Socialist society is seen as an independent entity, not simply as a foil to capitalist society, or as a refuge from its dilemmas—as with

93

those critical realists who have come closest to embracing socialism. Even more important is the treatment of those social forces
leading towards socialism; scientific, as against utopian, socialism
aims to locate those forces scientifically, just as socialist realism
is concerned to locate those human qualities which make for
the creation of a new social order. The revolt against the old
order, against capitalism—the point of contact between critical
realism and a socialist perspective—becomes a subordinate element in this wider context. Since perspective, as we have seen,
plays a decisive role as a selective principle in literature, these
considerations are of no small importance in forming the style of
socialist realism.

Let us consider our first point in greater detail—description
of socialism from the inside rather than from the outside. No
distinction between a superficial and a profound grasp of human
character is necessarily implied. Great satirists, such as Swift or
Saltykov-Shchedrin, always saw character from the outside. Indeed, this refusal to enter into all the subjective complexities of
the world they satirize is the presupposition of a good satirical
typology. The opposition I have in mind is different. By the
'outside' method a writer obtains a typology based on the individual and his personal conflicts; and from this base he works
towards wider social significance. The 'inside' method seeks to
discover an Archimedian point in the midst of social contradictions, and then bases its typology on an analysis of these
contradictions.

Many realistic writers use both methods; and both methods
may coexist in the same work of art. Dickens is a case in point:
his plebeian characters are explored from the inside, his upper-
and middle-class characters from the outside. Dickens is perhaps
an extreme case, but a most instructive one if we wish to study
the social origins of the phenomenon. It is evident that writers
will tend to present an inside picture of the class on which their
own experience of society is based. All other social classes will
tend to be seen from the outside. But, again, this is no more than
a generalization: Tolstoy's view of the world approximates to

that of the exploited Russian peasantry; yet he undoubtedly portrays the gentry, and a section of the aristocracy, from the inside.

On the other hand, only vulgar sociology conceives of class structure as something static. It is a dynamic thing, containing within itself past, present, and future of the society in question. There is a tendency for all writers to present the world of their immediate experience from the inside, and the past or future of that world (if the latter promises to be different from the present) from the outside. The great realists of course, vary in the range of their 'inside' knowledge. Shakespeare, no doubt, achieved the broadest range, depicting even the inside world of characters entirely unsympathetic to him. But many writers have deluded themselves as to their true position. Balzac's Quixotic *ancien régime* aristocracy is, unquestionably, a portrait from the inside. Yet it is a portrait done with devasting irony and critical detachment, not at all on a level with those of Alfred de Vigny or Achim von Arnim. Again, Balzac is wholly out of sympathy with his Mucingens or Gobseks; but they are drawn, nevertheless, from the inside.

With these reservations, it is clear that an 'outside' description of events in the past may attain a high degree of authenticity. In literature, as elsewhere, a critical understanding of the present is the key to the understanding of the past. In regard to the future, this is not necessarily so. In the preceding chapter I examined the modifications perspective underwent during the history of critical realism. We concluded that, for a correct assessment of the future, the perspective of socialism is necessarily increasing in importance. Yet, though this new perspective will help the critical realist to understand his own age, it will not enable him to conceive the future *from the inside*.

In socialist realism, this barrier is removed. Since its ideological basis is an understanding of the future, individuals working for that future will necessarily be portrayed from the inside. Here is the first point of divergence, then, between critical and socialist realism. Socialist realism is able to portray from the inside human beings whose energies are devoted to the building of a different future, and whose psychological and moral make-up is determined by this. The great critical realists failed to break through this barrier—there are many instances of this failure, from Zola's Etienne Lantier to Martin du Gard's Jacques Tibault. The description of Jacques Tibault as a child, and as a young man, is masterly. There are, too, successful episodes dealing with Tibault's socialist phase—particularly the love scenes in the Paris of August 1914. But the task of portraying Tibault's new socialist consciousness was beyond Martin du Gard's powers.

The explanation is to be found in the *concrete* nature of the new socialist perspective. I should perhaps say here what I mean by 'concrete', since we shall be concerned with the problem of its realization later on. Concreteness, then, in my sense, involves an awareness of the development, structure and goal of society as a whole. The great critical realists did, of course, at times achieve a comprehensive description of the totality of society. Yet there was an important period in the history of critical realism (i.e. before Walter Scott) when the writer was hardly aware of the historical nature of the reality he described. And even nineteenth-century historicism—which suffered a severe setback during the imperialist period—was deeply problematical. It was precisely where critical realism was most comprehensive and most profound—in the writings of Balzac and Tolstoy—that the historical diagnosis was most mistaken. Yet it permitted some extraordinary insights, both into man's social nature and into his role in history. The contrast was intensified in the imperialist period, following the decay of bourgeois historicism. Great realism was still possible—Thomas Mann is the obvious example—but it was at odds with its own ideology.

The perspective of socialism enables the writer to see society and history for what they are. This opens a fundamentally new, and highly fruitful, chapter in literary creation. Let us take two points. Socialist realism is a possibility rather than an actuality; and the effective realization of the possibility is a complex affair. A study of Marxism (not to speak of other activity in the

Socialist movement, even Party membership) is not of itself sufficient. A writer may acquire useful experience in this way, and become aware of certain intellectual and moral problems. But it is no easier to translate 'true consciousness' of reality into adequate aesthetic form than it is bourgeois 'false consciousness'.

Again, while it is true that a correct theoretical approach and a correct aesthetic (i.e. the creation of a typology) may often coincide, the methods and the results are not really identical. Their coincidence derives from the fact that both reflect the same reality. A correct aesthetic understanding of social and historical reality is the precondition of realism. A merely theoretical understanding—whether correct or incorrect—can only influence literature if completely absorbed and translated into suitable aesthetic categories. Whether the theory is correct or not is immaterial, since for a writer no theory, no conceptual understanding, can be more than a general guide. The relationship is indirect, dialectical; an erroneous, or partly erroneous, theory may nevertheless be a fruitful guiding principle. Lenin once remarked in a letter to Gorky, 'I am of the opinion that there is something in every philosophy which an artist can put to good use. . . .' And added, with Gorky's own work in mind, '. . . even if that philosophy be Idealistic'.

The reason is evidently that both approaches must grapple with the same infinite reality and endeavour to record their discoveries. Thus the most disparate approaches may yield fresh insights, and throw up new or hitherto neglected problems. Moreover, reality is neither static nor constant; the investigator cannot exhaust its substance. It is, on the contrary, a constant flux—only revealing a definite, though never simple, direction to the eye of the trained observer.

On the one hand, reality is forever throwing up new material, permitting older material to disappear from view. But the investigating subject, caught in its flux, is yet able to discover tendencies whose significance had not previously been understood. The development of new forms is intimately related to this active, unceasing exploration of reality. In this sense, there is certainly progress in art—although all works of art, whatever phase of development they belong to, are finally aesthetically equivalent. Schiller makes this point in his famous essay *Über Naive und Sentimentalische Dichtung*. Comparing the authors of Greek and modern literature—Shakespeare and Fielding are his examples—he concludes that the latter are superior in their treatment of women, and that this superiority reflects advances that have taken place in society. But he did not, of course, regard this as a criterion of higher aesthetic achievement.

A fuller understanding of the possibilities of human development, and of the laws underlying it, can form the basis of a new style—which in this sense, and only in this sense, will mark a higher stage in the development of art. Similarly, socialist perspective, correctly understood and applied, should enable the writer to depict life more comprehensively than any preceding perspective, not excluding that of critical realism.

To set out the points of contact and opposition between critical and socialist realism, I must recall our earlier discussion of the crisis of bourgeois literature. I need not refer to modernism in this place, since the opposition between it and socialist realism is evident. Earlier, we touched on an aspect of critical realism which served to illustrate the relation between it and socialist realism. I mean the role the revolutionary working class plays in modern society, without some account of which no picture of that society would be complete. I showed that critical realism was incapable of portraying this class and its problems from the inside. And I added that this was not the same thing as an inability to portray the past, and classes and groups existing in the past, from the inside.

Briefly, there are three possibilities. There is, first, the possibility of outright failure in an attempt to attack the new content directly (Roger Martin du Gard and, earlier, Zola). Secondly, there are cases where it has proved possible to evade the problem —Conrad, Sinclair Lewis—though the conditions which made

this possible are rapidly disappearing (consider the difference between colonialism today and in Conrad's time; consider Louis
Bromfield's attempt at a modern version of *Babbitt*). Or, thirdly,
the problems of our time may be presented wholly within
a bourgeois framework. The class struggle will be described from
the bourgeois point of view, its effects on society being demonstrated only indirectly, by revealing the psychological and moral
consequences. Thomas Mann is the great exponent of this
method. Yet it is evident—and nobody was more conscious of
this than Mann himself—that a literature accepting these presuppositions must be a literature of lowered vitality. It can never
aspire to the richness and fullness of a Fielding or a Gottfried
Keller; it will be the art of a society's old age. It will require hard
work, deep thought, and profound imagination to achieve, in
this roundabout way, the desired immediacy, to impose on
shrinking and reluctant material a new and satisfactory wholeness.

Socialist realism is in a position, on the other hand, both to
portray the totality of a society in its immediacy and to reveal its
pattern of development. Of course, neither socialist realism nor
critical realism are able to portray the totality of a society in the
crude sense of the word. Even Balzac, who set out to do this in
his *Comédie Humaine*, made this claim only in regard to the
whole cycle. Each part, novel or short story, contains only a
small segment, though complete in itself. But the greatness of
his conception is that the whole is constantly present in the
parts. Each individual novel is organically related to that whole;
the various, immensely complex motivations, interrelations and
combinations are embedded in an all-encompassing society. This
ambition to portray a social whole, found in most great realists
of the classical period, is inherited by socialist realism. Gorky's
Mother does not offer a straightforward depiction of capitalism.
Yet it would be wrong to compare this omission with, say,
Mann's omission of the theme of class struggle from *Dr Faustus*.
The latter presents only indirectly, through the career of one
bourgeois intellectual, the life of the proletariat; whereas Gorky's

99

novel, though it leaves out the bourgeoisie, focuses directly on the class struggle. Socialist realism, though it grapples with the same problems, is closer in its narrative method to the realism of the classical period, before realism was forced to adopt the indirect method of a Thomas Mann, than to the critical realism of our own time. Gorky, Sholokhov and others give proof of this.

Socialist realism's ambition to depict the totality of society is not, however, its specific stylistic criterion. It was not even that critical realism; even with Balzac there was the contrast between his grand conception and actual achievement. But socialist realism is certainly committed to the achievement of such totality more strongly than was critical realism. Not that the process of artistic realization is any less complex for that. In critical realism, as Zola's example shows, the ideal of a documentary totality, more suitable to the scientific monograph, was the product of certain inherent problems. I shall show that similar, and perhaps even greater, problems are inherent in socialist realism. The ideal of totality in art can never, of course, be more than a guiding principle, applied to a particular segment of life; it can never be more than an approximation to totality. Lenin demanded a similar dialectical conception of totality in regard to science: 'A problem can only be fully understood when all its aspects, all its implications, all its determinants, have been established and examined.' This demand applies even more to literature, where the achievement of depth, of intensive totality, always has priority over mere extensive totality.

From this it may appear that critical and socialist realism are virtually indistinguishable. But, in spite of the similarities, there are important qualitative differences. These derive from that hard-and-fast perspective of the future, that 'true consciousness', which socialist realism by definition possesses. This perspective enables the writer to obtain a fuller understanding of the life of the individual and of society than he could obtain elsewhere. Furthermore, a correct understanding of reality quickens the relation between theory and practice and gives rise to a new kind of human self-awareness: man becomes aware of his nature as an ineluctably social animal.

It is with the newness of this new content that we are concerned. New forms only result when such new phenomena enter human consciousness. Makarenko's *Didactic Poem* points to the unlimited formal possibilities inherent in the new content. In this respect, it is instructive to look at some of the best-known war novels. From *All Quiet on the Western Front* to *The Naked and the Dead* many honest, realistic novels of great aesthetic and ethical merit have been written. But war can only be understood in its totality if the writer has a perspective which enables him to understand the forces that lead to war, as Arnold Zweig had in *Education at Verdun* or A. Beck in *The Road to Volokamsk*. These latter works, far from giving us monographs on war, elevate the personal fate of their characters to the level of the typical; they mirror the totality of war in concrete relationships between typical, but living human beings.

Our account of the similarities between socialist and critical realism would be incomplete if the alliance between both these movements, and its historical necessity, were to be disregarded. The theoretical basis of this alliance is socialism's concern for the truth. In no other aesthetic does the truthful depiction of reality have so central a place as in Marxism. This is closely tied up with other elements in Marxist doctrine. For the Marxist, the road to socialism is identical with the movement of history itself. There is no phenomenon, objective or subjective, that has not its function in furthering, obstructing or deviating this development. A right understanding of such things is vital to the thinking socialist. Thus, *any* accurate account of reality is a contribution—whatever the author's subjective intention—to the Marxist critique of capitalism, and is a blow in the cause of socialism. In this sense, the alliance of socialism with realism may be said to have its roots in the revolutionary movement of the proletariat. A régime preparing for war, or a régime relying on oppression and confusion of the people, must necessarily

—as Mussolini, Hitler, and MacCarthy show—tend towards the suppression of realism.

But the alliance between critical and socialist realism is implicit also in the nature of art. It is impossible to work out the principles of socialist realism without taking into account the opposition between realism and modernism. In regard to the past, theoreticians of socialist realism are well aware of this; they have always considered the great critical realists allies in their struggle to establish the supremacy of realism in aesthetics. But the alliance is not merely theoretical. The historical insights in these writers' works, and the methods they used to achieve these insights, are vital to an understanding of the forces shaping the present and the future. They may help us to understand the struggle between the forces of progress and reaction, life and decay, in the modern world. To ignore all this is to throw away a most important weapon in our fight against the decadent literature of anti-realism. There were not a few modern critical realists, after all, who were allies of socialist realism in this fight—we have only to think of Romain Rolland.

Having established the existence of the alliance, we must show that the links between socialist realism and, say, Thomas Mann are not of a merely tactical kind; that socialist realism has a real claim to inherit the mantle of Goethe and Tolstoy. There are, of course, many examples of purely tactical collaboration. These came about frequently during the struggle against Fascism, and are to be found today again in the World Peace Movement. To apply the test of realism to these cases would be narrowly sectarian. Yet it is not easy to work out these distinctions in practice. Let us take the period between the wars, the period of Gide's and Malraux's short-lived left-wing sympathies. This alliance had no real ideological or aesthetic basis; it remained, consequently, no more than an episode. The World Peace Movement shows, again, that it is quite possible to distinguish between a writer's political stance and the character (realistic or otherwise) of his art. This is a point of some importance. Exaggerated claims were, of course, frequent at the time. During Gide's flirtation with socialism the anti-realistic elements in his work were conveniently overlooked; then, after the break, his significance in contemporary literature was belittled. But this does not mean that a solution to the problem is theoretically impossible.

The alliance between socialist and critical realism rests on deeper-reaching ideological premises. The most important is the proposition that socialist art is, of its nature, *national* art. I hasten to add that no sort of folk-mystique is implied in the phrase; still less any dogma about racial characteristics. It is just that any nation reflects the particular historical conditions through which it has passed. The decay of primitive communism took different forms in different places. Each European nation developed its own kind of feudalism. The decline of feudalism, the rise of capitalism, the particular structure of the working-class movement, however basically similar, differed importantly in different countries. An individual is born into a society that bears a specific physiognomy; his formative years are deeply influenced by its traditions; he is shaped by it as a thinking human being. And the great realist works of art are a main factor in creating the intellectual and spiritual climate which gives human personality its specifically national character. The stronger a writer's ties with the cultural heritage of his nation, the more original his work will be, even where he is in opposition to his own society and calls in a foreign tradition to redress the balance (Lessing and Shakespeare are a case in point. I have shown elsewhere how the influence of Tolstoy on Thomas Mann, Romain Rolland and Bernard Shaw helped to bring out specifically German, French and English characteristics in their writings.)

Today, critical and socialist realism are at one in their struggle against reactionary forces in politics and art. Lenin always insisted there was no Chinese Wall separating the bourgeois-democratic and proletarian revolutions. Equally, there is no such wall in the life of the individual, or in the community of writers. Gorky's development shows that the transition from a bourgeois-democratic view of the world to socialism may be gradual, almost intangible. Other bourgeois writers, such as Chekhov, display a similar pattern of transition, though Chekhov was never to cross the Rubicon. Thomas Mann was well aware of these transitional phases, experienced by the bourgeois writer who engages in self-criticism and glimpses the prospect of socialism on the horizon. In the twenties he wrote, in his *Paris Diary*: 'I am a bourgeois, certainly ... yet to understand the condition of the bourgeoisie today does imply a detachment from it, an awareness of the new forces. It is foolish to mistake self-awareness for quietism. Nobody who knows himself intimately remains the same man.' However intangible the transition, there must be still a qualitative break. But the fact that such transitions are possible, and their manifest importance for the development of socialist realism, shows that the alliance is deep and intimate.

No analysis of socialist realism would be complete without a consideration of the reactionary, decadent elements in social and literary life which influenced it in its early stages. The evolution of Johannes R. Becher and Bertolt Brecht, or of Paul Eluard and Louis Aragon, into socialist writers would have been unthinkable without German Expressionism and French Surrealism. But the matter cannot be left at that. None of these writers would have developed 'automatically' from his modernist beginnings into a socialist writer (though he may well have been a socialist in politics all along), had not certain countervailing forces been operative. They drew much strength, of course, both from their personal experiences and from sources outside the life of their own country—one has only to think of the impact of the Russian Revolution and, later, of the building of socialism in the Soviet Union. But the fact remains that these writers drew, for the most part, on their own national literature—it is enough to point to the influence of Heine and Hölderlin on Becher's development as a socialist poet. There can be no doubt that traditional bourgeois realism is a useful ally for the socialist writer.

Nobody can dispute that this is so. But what of the relation between critical and socialist realism in the period *after* the seizure of power by the proletariat? We must bear in mind that, however violent the political break, people (including writers) will not be automatically transformed. Lenin once remarked that socialism had to be built by people who were moulded by capitalism. The truth is, people are only transformed when they participate in the transformation of reality. The progressive bourgeois realist must not be expected to embrace socialism the moment the proletariat seizes power. Some progressive intellectuals—even those who later on become socialists—may be driven into the opposite camp by the experience of class struggle in its acutest form. And the upheavals to which a revolution gives rise may cause serious doubts even among long-standing supporters of socialism (consider Gorky's reaction during the period of acute class struggle in Russia).

Conflicts of allegiance in literature are likely to be more complex than in the practical fields of politics and economics. Curiosity, a delight in novelty for novelty's sake, a romantic anti-capitalism, may lead an extreme modernist to accept socialism. He may believe that his 'revolution of forms' is identical with socialist revolution, even its true expression. Again, sectarian communist intellectuals often fall for the dream of a 'proletarian culture', for the idea that a 'radically new' socialist culture can be produced, by artificial insemination as it were, independent of all traditions (proletkult). During the early years of the dictatorship of the proletariat in Russia such beliefs were rampant. The more level-headed communist theoreticians, Lenin in the lead, saw through these futile and basically anti-socialist ventures. But they could not be overcome before the new experience had been assimilated, before artists had understood the new forces at work in society and discovered how to give them artistic expression.

In view of this, it is not surprising that it took seventeen years —until after the 1st Congress of the Soviet Writers Union— for the term 'socialist realism' to become widely accepted. I will not describe in detail the preceding ideological discussion. The Congress's definition of the term (culminating in a famous paper read by Gorky) was the outcome of years of discussion between warring groups. The point of interest to us here is the new classi-

105

fication of 'fellow-traveller'. 'Fellow-travellers' are bourgeois writers, critical realists, who sympathize with, or at least acknowledge, the dictatorship of the proletariat and the goal of a socialist society. The term 'fellow-traveller' implies that the authorities of the time considered these writers allies in the making of a socialist literature. The decision was taken, I say, after many years of vehement discussion. The Central Committee resolution of 1925, acknowledging this alliance, was reversed by the RAPP group who acquired a dominating influence shortly afterwards. Soon, only 'explicitly' socialist writers were considered genuinely 'proletarian' (even Gorky and Sholokhov found themselves attacked). Only after the dissolution of RAPP in 1932 was the alliance re-affirmed, though there have been sporadic attempts since then to revive the RAPP ideology.

These ideological struggles in the Soviet Union illustrate our problem very well. But countries which became socialist later than the Soviet Union cannot simply adopt a formula of agreement reached after long and bitter ideological struggle. Lenin criticized again and again the sectarian assumption that the mass of the people could simply take over the intellectual vanguard's latest brainwave. In Lenin's view the masses can only be convinced of the truth of something when they have experienced it themselves. In this respect writers, too, belong to the masses, though they might not care to admit this. Literature depends on actual experience; resolutions, however well-meant, are no substitute for it. Soviet writers' experiences may shed light on the problem; but they do not provide a working model. The more so since, with the exception of China and Yugoslavia, none of the new socialist states owes its existence to civil war. In many respects, this development has its advantages. But there are also disadvantages. The shock-effect, the compulsion to make a decision which brings about a man's conversion, will be less pronounced in a mainly evolutionary process. Consequently, conversion presupposes more, not less political experience. I have not examined all the stumbling-blocks in the way of a bourgeois writer. But it is safe to conclude that many bourgeois writers, though sympathizing with socialism, will continue to work within the confines of critical realism.

Critical realism will therefore have a prolonged existence in the new socialist society. Some of the problems this raises we have dealt with already in a different context. First, there is that necessary precondition of critical realism even in capitalist society: not to reject the socialist perspective out of hand. This is still more necessary, of course, in socialist society. But here a dialectical shift is involved. As the perspective of socialism changes, as it is gradually translated into concrete reality, either the result will be growing approximation or, alternatively, a violent estrangement. Only a standstill is rare. Under socialism, the precarious balance familiar under capitalism gives way to more violent swings of the pendulum.

The second point concerns critical realism's inability to depict, from the inside, the social forces on which socialism is based. This is the case at present under capitalism. But it is far more critical for the writer who actually lives in a socialist society. Socialist reality confronts the critical realist with a society he is unable to describe from the inside. The fact that socialism is no longer a perspective, but has become the basis of his existence, makes it far more difficult for the bourgeois writer to evade the issue than it was for Thomas Mann. Is there, in fact, anything left for the critical realist to write about?

I would say: yes. We must not forget that remnants of the old order, and of the old consciousness, linger on and continue to inform many people's experience. But they do not survive—this is of crucial importance—in their old form. The character of any social phenomenon is determined by its orientation. A change of direction transforms not only the content and form of the phenomenon, it gives qualitatively new functions to that part of it which remains unchanged. Thus, the experiental material may seem familiar to the bourgeois writer; yet it has become, in fact, something altogether different. The writer is not simply called upon, as he was under capitalism, to relive, to re-explore historical change and development. He faces a quite

107

new task: he must apply to his raw material the concrete perspective of socialism—which he once saw as an abstraction—in order that he may grasp the new realities in their actual novelty, and not as elements of disintegration or decay. To a certain extent, this process is possible within the limits of bourgeois consciousness; but it will tend to lead a writer to develop closer ties with socialism. There will thus be a large body of literature combining socialist and critical realism—a point to which we must return. But, in any case, it is important to appreciate the value of works still being written in the critical realist tradition. For it was typical of the sectarian, bureaucratic narrowness of the Stalinist period that, in describing socialist reality, the need for a socialist perspective was continually overstressed. Dogmatists even went so far as to deny to any but socialist writers the right to point out difficulties or criticize mistakes. And these difficulties or mistakes had to be remedied instantly in the piece of writing in question. It was Lenin who maintained that the rights of the working population had often to be safeguarded against the bureaucratic depredations of their superiors. There is much scope, in any case, for critical realism in the emerging socialist society. It is a society in process of transformation; and change is reflected in different ways in different social groups. The assessment of such changes depends on the character of the group's contribution to the development of society as a whole. We have examined, if only in general terms, why critical realism in periods of transition is socially justified and desirable. But since genuine Marxism (not the bureaucratized, subjectivized version of it) is based on the exploration of objective reality, it must be in the interests of Marxism to enter into a close alliance with critical realism.

Clearly, the complexity of the new subject-matter will demand a variety of new forms. It is sectarian to expect every criticism to be accompanied by a solution, or to be based exclusively on communist principles. This would lead to a severe reduction of the scope of critical realism in socialist society. Critical realism is important because it can describe the reaction of the non-socialist to the new society, can depict its transforming power, its rich inherent complexity. Critical realism has thus a significant contribution to make to present-day literature and is an important ally of emerging socialism.

Our discussion has been concerned chiefly with the presentation of contemporary social reality. But topics from the recent or remote past also appear in a new light, since the building of socialism alters the perspective of every past event. It is a matter not simply of reappraising familiar material but of revaluing the entire historical scene, as the new perspective throws light on previously neglected phenomena. This is not to say that a writer who clings to bourgeois values will be unable to write about such things. Far from it. If his view of the world makes allowances for a socialist perspective, he will certainly be able to do so. For, though understanding the past in terms of the new socialist reality may represent, qualitatively speaking, an advance, no total break with traditional perspectives is required. Critical realism can excel at this kind of elucidation of the past.

Let me repeat Heine's adage: socialism is the most effective way of fighting the forces the bourgeois writer has always fought. The enemy, in Heine's time, was German Chauvinism. Later, it was aggressive Imperialism; still later, Fascism. Today, it is the ideology of the Cold War and the preparation for nuclear war. The fight against the common enemy, which has led to close political alliances in our age, enables the critical realist to allow for the socialist perspective of history without relinquishing his own ideological position. The less his historical material is concerned with the building of socialism, the wider will be the critical realist writer's scope. Not that matters closely related to socialism are necessarily beyond the grasp of critical realism. Each socialist movement has a particular national character. There is a close connection between a people's achievement of nationhood and its decisive class struggles. This connection determines not only a nation's particular fate, but also the character of its bourgeois and proletarian revolutionary movements. The evaluation of this process is, of course, properly the object of Marxist historiography. But literature, too, furnishes valuable insights.

The character of the alliance between critical and socialist realism should now be clear. The fact that bourgeois and, later, proletarian revolutionary movements often defended national interests against the ruling classes (e.g. the peasant revolts in Germany and Hungary in the sixteenth century, or the French Revolution) has not been adequately investigated by historians. Nor has it, moreover, become a part of the historical consciousness of the socialist. Though bourgeois writers often underestimate the social factor, every insight of this sort contributes to the socialist understanding of history, and to the understanding of national characteristics. This is important because many socialist realists neglect the national character of class struggles, stressing only their social nature. Since critical realism tends to concentrate on these aspects—somewhat one-sidedly—it may prove a valuable ally, contributing new insights and correcting the no less one-sided approach of socialist realism. A good example is the Hungarian writer Gyula Illyes' *The Dócza Tragedy*, which deals with the Hungarian peasants' revolt of 1514.

Then there is the question of the subjective experience of the individual writer. There can be no standstill in a writer's subjective development; to stand still, particularly in an age of crisis, is to retreat. I have pointed out the contradictions in the bourgeois intelligentsia's reaction to socialism. We have seen, too, that a purely negative reaction may put a writer out of touch with contemporary reality; it may reduce his perspective—rooted no longer in the present, but solely in the past—to a mere abstraction, and may prevent him imposing order on the human and social material at hand. The deeper the rift, the more tenuous will grow the links between the world as he sees it and objective reality, so that in the end he becomes alienated from what he should know most intimately. Such, often enough, is the fate of the emigré writer. So-called 'inner emigration' may be distinguished from emigration proper in that spiritual alienation is accompanied by social and political conformism and, frequently, by cynicism and hypocrisy. We have seen this to be the case with Gottfried Benn, Ernst Jünger and Ernst von Salomon (the fact that the mistakes, indeed crimes, committed in the Stalinist period seem to have confirmed points raised in this emigré literature, does not affect its position in the general historical development).

I have raised this more general sociological point in order to show up the essential contradictions inherent in any historical development. A writer's negative reaction to a historical phenomenon may have many motives. His reaction may, of course, spring from inability to understand the new phase of social development. But it may also be the justified rejection of a reactionary phenomenon. The two things should not be confused. Admittedly, this kind of rejection and an inability to understand new developments may go together. Take Vercors' *Le Silence de la Mer*, set during the German occupation of France. Though Vercors' rejection may be abstract, his historical perspective is based on real events and springs from an objective historical development. It would not be difficult to find other illustrations.

The problem acquires a new dimension when we examine the opposition between reactionary and progressive positions. The 'inner' and 'outer' emigrés from socialism are bound to lose contact with historical reality, whereas the emigré writers of the anti-Fascist period profited from their opposition, learning to understand certain historical processes better than before their emigration. Arnold Zweig and Leon Feuchtwanger were good examples of this; as were, of course, Heinrich and Thomas Mann.

The problems here are manifold and complex, but not insoluble. On the contrary, such conflicts can be extremely fruitful. In the transition period they form an important object of study: the relation of the bourgeois writer to socialist reality. It is striking that both bourgeois and socialist literature have shown a preference for the autobiographical *Bildungsroman*. This is no coincidence. Both types of society are, unlike earlier societies, in a state of constant, dynamic change. An individual growing up in them has to work things out for himself and struggle for a place in the community. The young Marx pointed out that there is something arbitrary about the individual's class status under capitalism. The bourgeois or proletarian is not a bourgeois or proletarian by birth; he becomes a member of his class in the course of his personal development—unlike in feudal society where class status is neither freely chosen nor alterable. It is clear that this mobility is even more pronounced in socialist society, which is a melting-pot of many classes, some of which will ultimately disappear, others of which will undergo substantial reorientation before the classless society is established. In socialist society the individual will enjoy greater freedom to choose a place for himself in society than under capitalism ('freedom' being understood here, of course, as conscious acceptance of historical necessity—a necessity which subsumes much that is apparently arbitrary).

Having pointed to the similarities, we must now also point to the differences. We have seen why the *Bildungsroman* plays an important part in both literatures. Hegel once formulated—with a cynicism recalling that of Ricardo—the social purpose of education under capitalism as follows: 'During his years of apprenticeship the hero is permitted to sow his wild oats; he learns to subordinate his wishes and views to the interests of the society; he then enters that society's hierarchic scheme and finds in it a comfortable niche.' In one sense, many of the great bourgeois novels contradict Hegel; in another, they confirm him. They contradict him inasmuch as the educational process does not always culminate in acceptance of, and adaptation to, bourgeois society. The realization of youthful convictions and dreams is obstructed by the pressures of society; the rebellious hero is broken, and driven into isolation, but the reconciliation with society of which Hegel speaks is not always extracted. On the other hand, since the individual's conflict with society often ends in resignation, the end-effect is not so different from what Hegel suggests. For society emerges triumphant, in spite of the hero's struggles.

In socialist society, the situation is different. A *Bildungsroman*, set in a socialist society, only apparently conforms to this pattern; experience itself will convert bourgeois individualist into social being. The end is not resignation. On the contrary, the process begins with resignation and leads on to active participation in the life of the community. Nor does the hero end up in isolation, as in so many of the later novels of critical realism. Rather, isolation gives way to an increasing involvement with the new social forces; a new and higher type of personality emerges. It is no accident that, whereas the typical bourgeois *Bildungsroman* takes its hero from childhood to the critical years of early adult life, its socialist counterpart often begins with the crisis of consciousness the adult bourgeois intellectual experiences when confronted with socialism. Both reflect reality. Under capitalism, we have to do with that element of arbitrariness which, as Marx showed, governs social existence. Under socialism, we have to do with the mental crisis which revolution represents for the bourgeois intellectual.

Particularly in the early phases of socialism, the main personal dilemma of the bourgeois intellectual—the decision for or against socialism—coincides with his dilemma as an artist. The coincidence can very well be stimulating. The energies released by his personal conflict with society strengthen his artistic efforts; whereas the correct formulation of his artistic problem may help the writer in his personal life. It is certainly striking how many novels of the early post-revolutionary period dealt with this crisis. It is even more striking that not a few writers were led to socialism through portraying this conflict, graduating from critical to socialist realism. The most interesting case is Alexei Tolstoy's powerful trilogy *Golgotha*, the first part of which was written in self-imposed exile, whereas the conclusion reflects a conscious acceptance of socialism. The same process can be observed in the writings of Fedin, Shaginyan and others.

During the transition period the dividing line between critical and socialist realism may not be drawn too rigidly. The two styles, distinguishable in theory, may well be found together in one work of art. This should not be surprising in the light of our previous investigations. We saw that for critical realism under capitalism a socialist perspective can prove a fruitful stimulus. Clearly, with the growing currency of socialist ideas once a socialist society is established, this fruitful influence will increase—until, finally, the distinction between the two is blurred. This development will run parallel with the development of the new society. At first, the dictatorship of the proletariat introduces socialization only in limited fields; even there, people do not always respond at once to the new developments. The new socialist institutions, that is to say, have to rely for a considerable period on people who, mechanically obeying its formulas, retain a bourgeois mentality. In other spheres—for instance in agriculture—the transformation process is even slower. Not only do bourgeois forms of social life persist for a long time, but the new forms taking their place do not always correspond to a socialist pattern.

The transitional forms between critical and socialist realism thus have parallels in the development of socialism. The critical realist, following tradition, analyses the contradictions in the disintegrating old order and the emerging new order. But he does not only see them as contradictions in the outside world, he feels them to be contradictions within himself; though he tends—again following tradition—to emphasize the contradictions rather than the forces working towards reconciliation. The elucidation of these contradictions (often overlooked or neglected by socialist realism), and the significance accorded to them, serve to strengthen the alliance between the two types of realism. Both work with the same material, but they apply themselves in different ways to the exploration of social reality. The deeper they probe, the closer will social reality approximate to the desired socialist society, and the closer will grow the ties between critical and socialist realism. In the process, the negative perspective of critical realism will gradually be transformed into a positive, socialist perspective.

As socialism develops, critical realism, as a distinct literary style, will wither away. We have pointed out some of the limitations, and the problems, facing the critical realist in a socialist society. We have shown that the scope of critical realism will narrow as a society comes into being the portrayal of which is beyond the grasp of the critical realist. The critical realist will increasingly apply perspectives approximating to socialist realism. This will gradually lead to a withering-away of critical realism. The expression 'withering-away' can be taken quite literally. Society will eventually achieve a condition which only socialist realism can adequately describe. It will be a protracted process—more protracted than impatient sectarians maintain—but the outcome is inevitable. Critical realism will wither away, as the literary forms of feudalism have withered away. Of course, individual efforts may influence the process, speed it up or hinder it; but the process is ultimately determined by social developments alone. Neither government decrees nor literary manifestoes will be of assistance. Indeed, the opposite. The surviving remnants of capitalism in human consciousness and society are hardly to be eliminated by such means.

All this argues the superiority—historically speaking—of socialist realism (I cannot sufficiently emphasize that this superiority does not confer automatic success on each individual work of socialist realism). The reason for this superiority is the insights which socialist ideology, socialist perspective, make available to the writer: they enable him to give a more comprehensive and deeper account of man as a social being than any traditional ideology.

Let me repeat, we are dealing with a potentiality, the realization of which depends on prevailing circumstances. The emergence of a new style is dependent on many external influences; and there is also a double internal danger which, in the history of literature, has often marked periods of transition. There may be a reluctance, on the one hand, to accept the logic of some new subject-matter; there may be a timid hanging-on to traditional styles, an unwillingness to give up old habits. There may also be, on the other hand, a tendency to overemphasize *abstract* aspects of new subject-matter ('in history', wrote Hegel, 'every new phenomenon emerges first in abstract form'). Abstraction then gains the upper hand. Concrete realities—the exploration with the help of the new consciousness of as yet unexplored subject-matter will be neglected or considered of secondary importance. In bourgeois literature, Voltaire's tragedies illustrate the first of these conditions; the plays of Lillo or Diderot the second.

These dangers beset socialist realism too. What is more, they are to be found at its point of greatest strength, in its new, more concrete, more comprehensive perspective. In practice, lack of boldness in grappling with the new perspective is the less common problem, and theoretically the easier to resolve. Of course, there will always be writers who shy away from pursuing things to their logical conclusions, who fall back on received standards. The result will be a diluted, inferior version of bourgeois realism, lacking the virtues of that tradition. The literature likely to be taken as a model will be that of the later bourgeois period (Zola, *Neue Sachlichkeit*, the 'documentary' etc.) rather than that of the classical period of critical realism. It would be wrong to confuse this with the kind of critical realism which, as we showed earlier, is the process of transition towards socialist realism. The decisive factor, as in our earlier discussion of the relation between modernism and critical realism, is not the particular commitment, but the general orientation to which this commitment points. Actually, retrograde tendencies are surprisingly common, as the recurring emphasis on 'documentary' description in socialist realist writings shows.

The second danger—an exaggeration of perspective—seems to me of much greater significance. In an address to the IVth German Writers' Congress I examined some of the salient features of this phenomenon. I argued that the concrete character of perspective was all too often disregarded. Writers mistook developmental tendencies—really no more than guiding principles for the present—for blueprints of the future. I pointed out in my address the aesthetic consequences of this misunderstanding. But it is no less vital today to investigate the ideological reasons for it; the more so since, in the light of the XXth Congress, the preceding period can now be seen in a clearer perspective. Although, where literature is concerned, many of the consequences have not yet been drawn.

I will start with what I consider the crucial question. In his last work on economics, Stalin sharply criticized that so-called 'economic subjectivism' which failed to see that socialist society, too, is determined by objective economic facts. Only the mastery of economic laws enables men to control their economic life. 'Economic subjectivism', however, attempts to apply those laws without regard to objective economic facts. Stalin here formulated a truth implicit in the Marxist classics. His attack on economic subjectivism was quite justified. But the tragic aspect of Stalin's career was that his own practice, and many of his pronouncements, helped to encourage economic subjectivism in the Soviet Union. The 'personality cult' was expressed often enough in Stalin's cavalier attitude to scientific facts and objective laws.

It is the method that concerns us here. In many cases Stalin's pronouncements may have corresponded with the truth; that is not our immediate concern. I wish to show that economic subjectivism was more than an accidental, short-lived aberration, corrected and criticized by Stalin in retrospect. Rather, it was the inevitable ideological consequence of the personality cult. In the field of economics the human will is confronted with hard facts. Ideology appears, on the other hand, a more pliable substance. And ideologies do prove, in fact, a good deal less obstinate than facts. Not only paper, in this respect, is patient—also stone: stone is indifferent to bad art as to good. The pliability is, of course, only apparent. Art too is governed by objective laws. An infringement of these laws may not have such practical consequences as do the infringement of economic laws; but it will result in work of inferior quality. Stalin's methods, therefore, met with much less resistance in the field of ideology than in the field of economics, where he often—shrewd as he was—gave in when resistance proved too strong. The natural sciences and technology were less vulnerable to the principles of economic

117

subjectivism than the social sciences and literature. In the latter a form of sectarianism arose which, though like that of earlier periods, was yet radically new. It will not do to trace back its origin to the *proletkult* and similar aberrations. We are confronted here with a phenomenon absolutely *sui generis*.

What were its essential features? I have pointed to the links with economic subjectivism. But there is a further point: if Marxist-Leninist objectivism is abandoned (though a nominal, subjectively sincere adherence to it may persist) the dialectical unity of theory and practice, of freedom and necessity, will be lost or dangerously weakened. The complex relationship between fundamental theory and everyday life, the day-to-day needs of political action, will be short-circuited.

The break-up of these mediating elements leads—in theory and in practice—to a false polarization. On the one hand, theory, from being a guide to practice, becomes a dogma, while, on the other hand, the element of contradiction between the two is eliminated. What we have is a polarization into dogmatism on the one hand, and pragmatism on the other. The former was widely discussed at the time of the XXth Congress. The latter has received rather less attention. It is nevertheless of great importance theoretically and practically. Marxism cannot be a guide to action if the relationship between perspective and actuality is subject to false simplification. But disregard for mediating elements leads to individual facts being seen without relation to the whole. Direct subsumption of facts under general, abstract principles will not alter this situation; for the transition between perspective and practice is then likely to be abrupt, and therefore unreal. And where facts are not distorted, but taken into due account, this is done in a pragmatic, and ultimately subjectivist, way.

Here again I shall confine myself to a general statement of the case: for we are concerned with the bearing of this theoretical constellation on literature. For literary purposes a correct, and not over-simplified, understanding of reality is clearly as vital as for pure theory. What the false polarization I have described implies, in literary terms, is an inability to overcome naturalism. There are many varieties of naturalism. Common to all is the weakening of the relation between ideological principle and individual fact. That is why pragmatism and empiricism have an affinity with naturalism. In socialist realism, once the dictatorship of the proletariat has been established, such tendencies to naturalism assume a special character. Bourgeois naturalism expressed the bourgeois writer's bafflement, his inability to discover a rational pattern in the multiplicity of facts. In socialist naturalism the polarization into dogmatism and pragmatism is the decisive ideological factor (in bourgeois literature, too, 'the facts' were sometimes presented in the naturalist manner, without mediation, and related directly to abstract generalizations: Zola was an exponent of this naturalism, as were Upton Sinclair and the writers of *Neue Sachlichkeit*). This polarization had to result in a false aesthetics. The mistake lay in bringing Marxism too directly to bear on practical, day-to-day problems. Marxism thus became something abstract. Day-to-day problems and their tactical solution are, of course, part of a larger reality. In the writing of the Stalinist period, however, the real problems were overlooked and—as with economic subjectivism—the correctness of particular solutions became a matter for dogmatism. Literature ceased to reflect the dynamic contradictions of social life; it became the illustration of an abstract 'truth'. The aesthetic consequences of such an approach are all too evident. Even where this 'truth' was in fact true and not, as so often, a lie or a half-truth, the notion of literature-as-illustration was extremely detrimental to good writing.

The tendency to use literature as an illustration was paralleled by another fallacy. This involved a reversal of the correct relation between research, propaganda and agitation. Instead of basing propaganda on research, thus forging propaganda into a powerful instrument of agitation, agitation became the point of departure, the guiding principle of propaganda and research. Both were thus condemned to petrification and reduced in scope and effectiveness.

119

Agitation became, too, the regulative principle of literature. Of course, there has always been a type of literature passionately engaged in day-to-day political issues. It will, let us hope, continue to exist, and there is no reason why it should not aim at artistic perfection. But it is disastrous to subsume all literature under this head. Writers must be allowed to find their own point of contact with day-to-day politics, and be allowed to work out, as did Mayakovsky and Petöfi, suitable means of dealing with it. This is radically different from Stalinist literature-as-illustration, based on the requirements of agitation.

Let me take a specific example. The decisive distinction between socialism and all previous societies is that socialism aims to eliminate the antagonistic character of social contradictions. Literature has the immensely important task of describing this process, of exploring the problems thrown up by it, of showing how some traditional problems disappear and others are modified (I have dealt with these points elsewhere, particularly in my study of Makarenko). If, however, the elimination of this antagonistic character is seen as something immediately realizable, rather than as a process, both the antagonism and the contradiction, the motor of all development, will disappear from the reality to be depicted. That I am right in this is suggested by the fact that a few years ago official Soviet literary criticism launched an attack on the so-called 'drama-without-conflict'. Yet it was not only Soviet drama, but also Soviet novels, short stories and poetry that were emptied of conflict in that period.

This is not the only case in which dogmatic sectarianism in literature has come in for criticism. We have already cited Stalin's critique of economic subjectivism. But did these criticisms really get to the root of the problem? I think not. Though extreme cases of 'literature-without-conflict' were condemned, the doctrine of the priority of agitation over literature was adhered to. Now, in political life, the good agitator must be able to give an immediate answer to a question. But if he is prudent he will point out that the solutions to some problems require time. Many writers have lacked this prudence and literary criticism has applauded them for it. Thus, a writer wishes to describe some problem in socialist society. But he also feels it to be his duty to offer a complete solution to the problem, within the framework of his work of art. There is, let us say, a speculator living in a certain village. He must be instantly converted or punished, it goes without saying. The fact that in an emergent socialist society there are still antagonistic contradictions is ignored by these writers. They do not see that the non-antagonistic character of contradictions only gradually prevails, and that even in the socialist society there may be insoluble conflicts. Nor do they see that neglect of existing contradictions —even if non-antagonistic in character—is liable precisely to render these contradictions antagonistic. What is involved is more than an impoverishment of literature in the face of the new reality. Since they fail to grasp the dialectical structure of these new non-antagonistic contradictions, their picture of the new reality will be distorted. Instead of a dialectical structure we shall get a static schematism. Here again, the new naturalism is rooted ideologically in Stalinism. Nor is it surprising that it should be found together with a false revolutionary romanticism.

This brings us to the distinction between a justified historical optimism—which can prove immensely fruitful—and that schematic optimism which gives rise to the 'happy ending'. I dealt with this problem in my study of Sholokhov's *Virgin Soil*, showing that many bourgeois critics' attacks on the optimism of socialist realism are due to an inability to understand the new developments. I pointed out that even where these attacks are justified, the 'happy ending' is qualitatively different from that in bourgeois literature. I examined the schematism common to both and pointed out the differences: 'These instances do not constitute a conscious falsification of social reality ... they represent an illegitimate simplification of its development. ... Historical optimism is degraded into a merely schematic optimism. The reader reacts to this with the same distaste as he does to a bourgeois "happy ending", though the method is not comparable.'

I have nothing to add to this formulation. Schematism was the consequence of an attitude that could not, so long as it predominated, be tackled by criticism of individual points—which was, indeed, never lacking and often correct in diagnosis.

Let us consider one or two concrete instances. Fadejev repeatedly—and, as I believe, rightly—pointed out that there were always superfluous characters in Soviet novels. This was certainly the case. What was the reason? It can be found, I believe, in the political and aesthetic situation produced by the dogmatism of the Stalinist period. If a writer feels obliged, like an agitator, to supply ready solutions to all the political problems of the day, his work will suffer. He will not be able, raising human conflicts to the level of the typical, to shed new light on the decisive problems of the age, as did Balzac or Tolstoy. For the complexity of such conflicts does not allow of the establishment of direct links between abstract principle and concrete fact. The writer analyses his problem theoretically and thinks up suitable characters to 'illustrate' it. The result is aesthetically disastrous. His composition consists of a pseudo-artistic superstructure resting on a preexistent theory. Such work fails by the standards of realistic art, as Fadejev discovered. Many of the illustrative characters are gratuitous, irrelevant to the action—merely forming part of the theoretical conception. Failure was not due to lack of talent or artistic negligence—quite a few of these novels were the work of talented writers—but to misconceived artistic principles.

We have already touched on the problem of typology. What is the key to these 'typical' heroes of literature? The *typical* is not to be confused with the *average* (though there are cases where this holds true), nor with the *eccentric* (though the typical does as a rule go beyond the normal). A character is typical, in this technical sense, when his innermost being is determined by objective forces at work in society. Vautrin or Julien Sorel, superficially eccentric, are *typical* in their behaviour: the determining factors of a particular historical phase are found in them in concentrated form. Yet, though typical, they are never crudely 'illustrative'. There is a dialectic in these characters

122

linking the individual—and all accompanying accidentals—with the typical. Levin was typical of the Russian land-owning class at a period when everything was 'being turned upside down'. The reader learns his personal peculiarities and is sometimes tempted to consider him, not wholly wrongly, as an outsider and an eccentric—until he realizes that such eccentricities are the mark of an age in transition.

The heroes of that schematic literature I have described altogether lack these features. They are not typical, but topical. Their features are prescribed by a specific political intention. I should add that it is always extremely difficult to isolate 'typical' features. The typical hero reacts with his entire personality to the life of his age. Whenever socialist realism produces authentic types—Fadejev's Levinson, or Sholokhov's Grigory Melyekov—there is present this organic unity of profound individuality and profound typicality. The characters produced by the schematists, on the other hand, are both above and beneath the level of typicality. The individual characterization is beneath it (whereas Natasha Rostova's 'tripping step', say, or Anna Karenina's ball costume are unquestionably typical), whereas what is intended to establish their typicality may be irrelevant to their psychological make-up. This weakness is common, of course, to all naturalistic literature—Zola's 'typical' characters have similar shortcomings.

The same circumstances that produce these tendencies in socialist realism also have other effects. What is socially typical, and what is not? Economic subjectivism and sectarian dogmatism were guilty of the mechanical application of a political conception of the type in literature. In politics, the typical is in opposition to the exceptional and the individual. In a particular historical period one phenomenon can be represented by one type only; the political character of the period is implicit in the distinction between the type and the multiplicity of untypical phenomena. In regard to the First World War, Lenin made this distinction with decisive clarity; the war was the typical product of imperialism. Criticizing those who maintained that national wars were impossible in the age of imperialism, he stated that 'an age is the sum of many phenomena; it contains not only typical, but many other components'.

Art and literature, however, require a multiplicity of typical phenomena. The merest by-products of a phase of evolution may qualify as artistic types; this may be necessary for the work of art to be of lasting value. While in science (and politics) the typical and the untypical are strictly opposed, there is no authentic fictional character who is not typical in one way or another. What in nature is no more than an individual particularity may become typical in its literary presentation. The hierarchy of the compositional pattern gives a different, but no less truthful picture of reality than does natural science. That is why the dogmatic, mechanical application of political concepts in art must be dangerously restrictive. Particularly so if dogmatism, as in the Stalinist period, distorts reality by its subjectivist approach and expects the artist to adopt its own arbitrary typology. The use of this kind of typology is sufficient explanation of the rigidity and anaemia of socialist naturalism.

So far, we have concentrated on the drawbacks of this naturalism. In the nineteen-twenties, Franz Mehring, the German Marxist literary critic, showed in a perceptive study of German Naturalism how its shortcomings had led to its being supplemented by a special kind of romanticism. Indeed, one could say that romanticism (not the historical kind which arose at the beginning of the nineteenth century in reaction to the French Revolution, but the vague, generalized kind with which we have since become familiar) was the 'guilty conscience' of Naturalism. This formulation, of course, meets only the emotional and artistic side of the question. But it helps to account for the popularity of the slogan at different periods under very different conditions. It cannot, of course, explain the actual social origin of the tendency. We must now ourselves enquire into this, bearing in mind the importance of the emotional factor, the 'guilty conscience', for the dissemination of romantic attitudes.

We all know that 'revolutionary romanticism' has been, for

the last two decades, one of the hall-marks of socialist realism. How was it that romanticism—for all the attractiveness of the accompanying epithet—suddenly became part of Marxist aesthetics, although Marx and Lenin never used the term save with ironic contempt? To my mind, it has the same cause as Naturalism in socialist writing: the economic subjectivism and voluntarism produced by the personality cult. Revolutionary romanticism is the aesthetic equivalent of economic subjectivism.

The reasons are evident: economic subjectivism confuses what is subjectively desirable with what is objectively there. It reduces perspective, as we saw, to the level of practical day-to-day exigency. Life is thus robbed of its poetry. For the poetry of life lies in life's wholeness and self-sufficiency. This 'poetic' quality is inherent in all human development, in a man's individual fate, in growth and change. It reveals itself also in the 'slyness' of reality, of which Lenin used to speak—implying that the laws of existence are more complex than thought can easily express, and the realization of these laws a process so involved as to elude prediction. That profound awe in the face of experience we find in great minds—Leonardo or Lenin, Goethe or Tolstoy—is based on this knowledge. As is the enduring spell of all works of art that evoke life's inexhaustible dynamism.

Naturalism, socialist or otherwise, deprives life of its poetry, reduces all to prose. Naturalism's schematic methods are incapable of grasping the 'slyness' of reality, its wealth and beauty. That naturalism destroys the poetry of life is widely recognized, even by those critics and writers who have helped to bring about this state of affairs. Characteristically, public opinion in the socialist countries was never as vain of socialist naturalism as were bourgeois intellectuals of their modernism. But during the Stalinist period, as we know, many crucial Marxist doctrines were misrepresented. Literary theoreticians, therefore, thought up a poetical substitute for naturalism, 'revolutionary romanticism', instead of attempting an ideologically correct aesthetic solution.

Once again, the decisive error is the misconception of perspective, its equation with reality. This fallacy, which had produced the naturalistic de-poetization of reality in the first place, was now employed to turn back prose into poetry. To provide a theoretical basis, Marxism had to be interpreted voluntaristically, in the manner of economic subjectivism. According to Marx, the poetry of the socialist revolution cannot draw its inspiration from the past, as did that of the bourgeois revolution, but only from the future. Because of this orientation the proletarian revolution must, as Marx put it, practice permanent self-criticism of a thoroughness 'bordering on cruelty'. At the time of the Paris Commune, Marx formulated the duty of the revolutionary working-class as follows: 'This class is not concerned with putting ideals into practice. Its business is to bring to birth those new elements in the womb of decaying bourgeois society.' The poetry of the future demands, in Marx's eyes, sober and inexorable criticism of the forces leading—in actuality, not only in imagination—towards socialism. The poetry of the future is the means by which the character of the present can be understood in its own particularity. This notion of Marx is so clearly opposed to romanticism that further discussion may be dispensed with. It is not accidental that Marx should always have opposed romanticism and held Shakespeare and Balzac, the 'cruelly' critical realists, to be the masters of post-classical literature.

The theoreticians of revolutionary romanticism often refer to Lenin's saying, in his early work *What is to be done?*, that revolutionaries 'must dream'. Mistakenly. For Lenin always distinguished sharply between perspective and reality, even while pointing out their interdependence. He mocked the empiricists who got bogged down in day-to-day problems; who, like Eduard Bernstein, played off the 'ultimate goal' against the 'movement'. Lenin's 'dreaming' is simply that profound, passionate vision of a future which it is in the power of realistic revolutionary measures to construct. This 'dreaming' adds a new dimension to every revolutionary act, however insignificant. But only if that act is based on a correct understanding of objective reality, taking into account the complexity, the 'slyness' of reality. Lenin quotes some remarks of Pissarev's to the effect that dreaming is a healthy, life-enhancing activity—and uses them to make fun of his opponents. The true criterion of health, he says, is that the 'dreamer should observe life attentively, compare his observations with his phantasies, and devote his efforts diligently to the realization of his dreams'. Again, it is no accident that Lenin, like Marx, should regard Tolstoy's realism—in spite of its apparent ideological shortcomings—as a model for the literature of the future.

The 'dreams' of revolutionary romanticism are the direct opposite of what Lenin called for. Poetry, certainly, has the right to anticipate the future in imagination. Nor is this the exclusive privilege of lyrical poetry. In the works of revolutionary poets such 'dreaming' has always played an honourable role. But it is no less legitimate for characters in novels or plays to indulge in musing. Take the dream of young Nicolai Bolkonsky, which concludes Tolstoy's *War and Peace*. Its perspective is that of the Decembrist conspiracy of the eighteen-twenties, thus linking the novel with the progressive traditions of Russian history. Yet perspective and reality are carefully differentiated. The dream of Nicolai Bolkonsky can only afford us these glimpses of the future because we have already been introduced—through Pierre's Petersburg activities and his friends' reactions to them—to contemporary social movements. We must not forget that poetry also contains both components: description of reality and perspective. Poetry, to be successful, cannot feed on unfettered subjectivity. Its point of departure is life itself, and its particular mode of reflecting reality is governed by the same artistic laws as the novel and the drama. Where this structure is lacking, the poet's dreams disintegrate into those fragmentary perceptions of life, common, for instance, in German Expressionism. In contrast, the young Brecht's magnificent, hate-inspired 'Ballad of the Dead Soldier' draws its strength from a correct relationship between perspective and reality.

We have seen how economic subjectivism proved doubly fatal in the literary field. It limited, on the one hand, the portrayal of reality to a crude naturalism; and introduced, on the other, a false substitute in the shape of revolutionary romanticism. (I would like to mention, in this context, a point not directly related to our examination. The same tendencies led to a distortion of Lenin's concept of 'partisanship'. Lenin, in attacking Struve's notion of objectivism, showed that Marxism combines a profounder, richer objectivity with a conscious subjective 'partisanship'. Under Stalin objectivity was outlawed as 'objectivism', and its place taken by a wholly subjectivized 'partisanship'. The link with economic subjectivism is plain. It is plain, too, that this must lead to the erection of an insurmountable barrier between critical and socialist realism.)

A further factor was the particular kind of perspective employed. Stalin proclaimed two—erroneous and mutually exclusive—perspectives. First, there was the dogma that the class struggle would continue, and indeed gather momentum; the XXth Congress has succeeded in correcting this view. Stalin's second perspective was the dogma that communism, the second phase of socialism, was imminent. He tried to reconcile these two contradictory propositions by revising the Marxist doctrine of the withering-away of the state: communism would be brought about in spite of the capitalist encirclement of the only existing socialist state. The stage of 'from everyone according to his abilities, to everyone according to his needs' would be reached while the state, the political police and the rest were still in being.

The world of literature is concrete. A perspective of so heterogeneous and contradictory a nature is of no use to it. Indeed, the two components of this perspective were frequently applied separately, much to the detriment of the works in question, since it broke their unity. Stalin's dogma of the increasing violence of the class struggle led to a conspiracy theory of politics. The logical culmination was the Moscow purge trials, where all the contradictions of the developing Soviet system were blamed on the activities of spies and counter-revolutionaries. These monstrous violations of legality and elementary justice were based on grotesque reasoning. All the difficulties and conflicts that arose during the building of socialism might have been avoided, according to this line of argument, if the security organs had done a better job and if Bukharin, Sinoviev, and the rest had been got rid of in 1917! In literature the adoption of this view led to a tedious schematism: difficulties in the building of socialism were invariably blamed on the activities of enemy agents. The exposure of these agents served as the denouement of the plot as well as the solution of the conflict. Both before the agent's arrival, and after his exposure, there existed an idyllic state of non-conflict. Naturally, there will be spies and counter-revolutionaries as long as two rival social systems exist. But these elements only use for their own criminal purposes existing difficulties, contradictions and mistakes. The perspective proclaimed by Stalin encouraged writers to attribute all evils to these 'enemies'. They were seen as not merely profiting from existing difficulties, but as actually creating them. It was in fact a deus-ex-machina solution—true to the spirit of the personality cult. Instead of the genuine tension underlying the struggle for socialism, we got the artificial tension of a detective story. Since these works relied on purely artificial effects, they were incapable of reflecting reality truthfully and were often extremely implausible. Their narrow, flat naturalistic psychology was then artifically enriched, and theoretically legitimated, by the introduction of revolutionary romanticism.

The perspective of imminent communism had a double effect on the psychological, moral, and typological structure of the novel. On the one hand, events which were still exceptional at that stage of socialism, were presented as typical. Thus, an otherwise interesting novel would be fatally marred by a scene in which a woman on a collective farm rejected the prize of a lamb she had herself brought up because communal is dearer to her heart than private property. Or a group of young Komsomols set out to win a harvest competition; they succeed in this by giving up their lunch-hour—only the strict orders of the supervisor can make them take some food and have a proper rest. The supervisor regards their zeal as an indication of the imminence of communism. Yet we are told that this collective farm is situated in a backward part of the country.

In criticizing revolutionary romanticism I am not concerned with the factual truth of such scenes. I only ask whether they can be considered 'typical'. From an artistic point of view, they are clearly not typical, as they are not presented as exceptional cases. They are presented as the average, the norm. But nor are they typical in the political sense of the word. They are there to illustrate an abstraction, the erroneous dogma of the imminence of communism. This is no more than wishful thinking; the characters and situations are not taken from life, they are abstract, bloodless, blurred. But the dogma of revolutionary romanticism claimed a higher reality for these false, untypical images of reality. Faulty theory may provide an excuse for these failures, but it will never make these works artistically convincing.

Lenin, and to a certain extent Stalin, considered it vital in the transitional period to awaken in the working population a personal interest in their work (by means of bonuses and differential pay). And one of the points in the XXth Congress' criticism of the past was that the socialist education of the population had been badly neglected. The 'typical' situation is, thus, that men have to be educated for socialism. Yet the literature we are criticizing abounds with types anticipating the imminent establishment of communism. Socialist consciousness is taken for granted; it is only a step to the achievement of communist consciousness. Of course, there may be genuine examples of this. At times these examples may even assume a symptomatic, and thus 'typical' significance. The periods of historical development are not, as in metaphysical speculation, to be rigidly distinguished. But it requires not only an increase in production so great that each can consume according to his needs (not according to his work, as in socialism) to achieve communism. There is also that new morality which, as Marx said, sees in work not just a means for ensuring the necessities of life, but 'one of the requirements of life itself'.

Naturally, this new attitude to work—and the increase in

production—will begin to take shape under socialism, and will gradually lead to communism. The emergence of characteristics anticipatory of the future may form the subject-matter of contemporary literature, and be presented as typical. But this is only possible if, as I showed in regard to naturalism, the specific ambience of such phenomena is conveyed. Here, the method used by Chernichevsky in his *What is to be done?* seems to me instructive. Chernichevsky's intention was to delineate the New Man. In Lopukhov, Kirsanov, Vera he confronts the reader with average representatives of the new reality who, basing their behaviour on a rational egotism, are out to overcome the contradictions inherent in the old order. On the other hand, there is the heroic figure of Rakhmetov, the revolutionary working for the overthrow of antiquated social institutions. Both are seen as types, and the typology is cleverly related in the writing to social and historical developments. Naturalism, as we have seen, cannot place its typology successfully in social reality. And revolutionary romanticism, by taking over the schematic, ahistorical typology of naturalism, is a substitute for poetry whose main effect is to accentuate the schematism of naturalism.

The notion that men should be given an incentive, a personal interest in their work, is no mere tactical device. It expresses the non-ascetic character of scientific socialism, in contrast to the asceticism of its primitive beginnings, and of its later sectarian aberrations. In the 1840's, the young Engels already saw the importance of this problem, examining it in a letter to Marx on the occasion of Max Stirner's newly published *The Individual and his Property*. Of interest to us is not so much Engels' brilliant refutation of Stirner's theory, but his vehement attack on Moses Hess who, in his ascetic Idealism, had minimized the role of egoism in social development and in socialist theory. In Engels' view, the only valid element in Stirner is his understanding of the role of egoism. Let me quote a crucial passage: 'What is valid is the idea that we have to make a cause our own before we are prepared to work for it, that, in this sense, apart from any hope of material gain, we are communists out of egoism, are human beings—and not merely individuals—out of egoism. . . . If we take the living individual being as the basis, the starting-point for our image of the humanity, egoism—not Stirner's "rational egoism" alone, but our egoism of the heart—will be the ground of our love of humanity and give it sound roots.'

In every phase of socialist development, asceticism of one kind or another has made its appearance. As a phenomenon, it is contradictory. Its subjective motive may be of the noblest; its role, particularly in a revolutionary situation, may be admissible, indeed exemplary. Yet we cannot ignore the reactionary elements, in terms of socialist education, that it contains. That is why the ascetic attitude has been constantly criticized within the socialist movement. Examples in Soviet literature might be the 'ascetic' Nagulnov, criticized in Sholokhov's *Virgin Soil*, or the Levin criticized in Platonov's story *The Immortal Ones* (I refer the reader to a detailed analysis of this problem in my *Russian Realism and World Literature*). Another example is Julius Fucik, whose posthumous writings give evidence of an anti-ascetic heroism. And the same is true of many letters written by victims of Fascist terror.

It is important, in regard to the recent past, to see the problem of asceticism in proper perspective. Under 'bureaucratism', that typical by-product of Stalin's personality cult, asceticism acquired a special significance. It was imposed on the population by bureaucrats who were not inclined to adhere to it themselves. This aberration will no doubt disappear with the elimination of the personality cult and the establishment of socialist democracy.

The personal, 'egoistic' interest in work should be seen in a wider ideological context. It is really part of the struggle for the development of a full human personality—an indispensable element in it, as Lenin recognized. Revolutionary romanticism, by neglecting decisive facts as 'beneath its vision', (just as naturalism ignored them as 'above its vision'), contributed to that oversimplifying schematism which has distorted the actual grandeur of the spectacle of emergent socialism.

I must stress that my criticism is not directed towards all

132

socialist literature. Plainly, Gorky (in *Klim Samgin*), Sholokhov, Makarenko, Alexei Tolstoy, Trenov, Fedin, Anna Seghers, Tibor Dery and many others never fell into these errors. Certainly, the artistic greatness of a particular movement is always, and rightly, judged by its highest achievement; the merely average sinks into well-deserved oblivion. To discuss Elizabethan drama is to discuss Shakespeare, or at most a few of his major contemporaries, but not Middleton or Tourneur. To assess early nineteenth-century realism we have to concentrate on Balzac and Stendhal, not on those novelists who received equal, if not greater, attention at the time. Only if we bear this in mind, can we appreciate the epoch-making significance of socialist realism.

Socialist realism has still to fight to establish its international reputation. In the field of the arts, true coexistence, the exchange of ideas between representatives of different cultures, depends on mutual good-will. Discussion must concentrate on what is in common, however opposed the parties may otherwise be. This common basis, as far as socialist realism is concerned, is very slight. The blame for this rests mainly with the Cold War ideologists, who are out to discredit everything to do with socialism. But those theoreticians of modernism are also to blame for whom all literature must bear the stamp of decadent formalism. Slanderous attacks and misrepresentations can only, we should remember, be countered by an appeal to objective truth. And the truth about socialist realism is that its content and form were seriously distorted during the Stalinist period. It is necessary, therefore, not only to point out these artistic errors and their ideological origins, but to draw a strict line between genuine socialist realism and the works that suffer from these distortions.

It would be slanderous to assert that during the Stalinist period socialist democracy, or the socialist basis of economic construction, were totally destroyed. Yet the true face of socialism can only re-emerge if the forces working against it during past decades are eliminated. That, indeed, is one purpose of this investigation. To obtain recognition for the genuinely achieved successes of socialist realism, greater efforts must be made to distinguish between the distortions and the novel and constructive features.

What is the connection between our present analysis of these unfortunate developments in socialist realism and our previous discussion of the relationship between critical and socialist realism in a socialist society? The connection, I think, is very real. We have seen that naturalism and romanticism inhibited socialist writers' self-criticism in the face of socialist development. The 'slyness' of the contradictions it contains, its overcoming of internal and external opposition, its gradual progress towards the ultimate goal—all this was concealed by a superficial schematic subjectivism. Yet it was precisely the searching-out of contradictions, the revelation of history's labyrinthine course, that was the greatness of critical realism. That is why it can assist socialist realism in finding a cure for its self-inflicted wounds.

It must be said in justice that both socialist literature and socialist criticism have acknowledged this situation. There have always been those who recognized the aesthetic failings of much socialist realist writing, pointed to the mastery of the great critical realists of past and present, and recommended the study of their works to socialist writers. But this was a matter of instinct rather than of rational understanding. The superficial reasons for this mastery were seen, but the real reasons left unexplored. What was admired was often no more than technical proficiency or sophistication. I have tried to show that the reasons for this mastery of the great realists lie deeper than technical virtuosity. A writer's greatness springs from the depth and richness of his experience of reality. The study of the masters of past and contemporary critical realism will have to focus on the depth of these masters' experience; and the lessons learnt will be a subtler and more profound understanding of reality. Only then will the writer be in a position to develop his own talent, to seek the specific artistic form adequate to his specific content. This notion of literary mastery all the great realists have in common;

Goethe and Gorky have described in their autobiographies how this fruitful interrelation of life and literature comes into being.

I take this, then, to be the basis of any useful alliance between critical and socialist realism. The situation in the Soviet Union is different from that of societies which have more recently begun to move towards socialism. There, most of the critical realist writers have already adopted socialist realism. Socialist realism has produced a range of masterpieces, rooted in a socialist understanding of reality. For the Soviet writer, the alliance between critical and socialist realism has acquired the wider significance of a critical evaluation of the whole literary heritage. This need not prevent him, of course, from entering into an alliance with critical realists working in other socialist, or non-socialist countries.

The situation is different in the newer socialist states where there are still important representatives of critical realism. To tell the truth—and sincerity is the basis of any alliance—the sectarian schematism of the Stalinist period did much to alienate critical realist writers from socialism. Many socialist writers developed that 'communist arrogance', which Lenin so often attacked, that complacency which the ideological sectarianism and artistic narrowness of the Stalinist period supported and justified. In this atmosphere many critical realist writers stopped writing, or made concessions against their better judgment. And there were some writers, driven into opposition to socialism, whose artistic development was thereby seriously compromised.

The discussions which the XXth Congress has set going, and the profound changes these discussions have already brought in their train, will surely contribute to the break-up of dogmatism, and the establishment of a working alliance between critical and socialist realism. With the growth of socialist democracy, and the evolution towards genuinely national varieties of socialism, this alliance will deepen. The living traditions of critical realism have an important role to play in plotting the complex paths of socialist development.

SUMMER 1956.

Index